THE SELBY PRINTOUT

THE SELBY PRINTOUT

A Novel

by

Ruth Benjamin

TARGUM/FELDHEIM

Published by:
Targum Press, Inc.
22700 W. Eleven Mile Rd.
Southfield, MI 48034

Distributed by:
Feldheim Publishers
200 Airport Executive Park
Nanuet, NY 10954

Distributed in Israel by:
Targum Press Ltd.
POB 43170
Jerusalem 91430

DEDICATION

To
Rabbi Yisroel and Sara Feige Shusterman
and their family

And to my family
Uzi, Devorah, Chaya, Dovi, Rivky, Lozzy, and Nechama
Shinan, Tzefon HaShomron, Israel

Yirmy, Rivky, and Esty van Halem, Brooklyn, New York

Yosef Yitzchok, Sara Dina, and Rikal Levy
Brooklyn, New York

And to my late husband
Dr. Boroch Dovber Benjamin, *z"l*

With special thanks to
Rabbi Mordechai Abraham, who shared his experiences
of being bitten by a puff adder in the Drakensberg area

CHAPTER 1

The man found his hands trembling a little as he keyed in the number. Would it work? Had he really cracked the code? Could he log in and operate the other accounts? Had he really discovered the "back door" to the system? He had been working on it long enough. Hopefully this would be a breakthrough. He was sure he could bypass all the passwords.

He hardly dared look at the screen in front of him, but on the other hand, could he resist it? Something told him that nothing had changed. He looked up, disappointed. It was the usual message:

```
ACCESS TO SYSTEM DENIED
```

He sighed. Would it never work? He reached for a drink, downing it with one gulp. Why wasn't it working? Why wasn't he getting into the system? He was sure he had managed to do it this time. What could be wrong? He tried again with the same result. Why did these things have to be so complicated?

He poured himself another drink. How much longer would he have to work on this? He didn't have forever. He had to do it soon, very soon.

Suddenly remembering something, he took out a disk from his pocket, turning it over several times. This surely was the one he had downloaded from the Internet. How could it work? How could someone know how to get into an unfamiliar system, some stranger so many miles away? But what did he have to lose? He activated the modem and waited.

Connecting...connecting. Was the software authentic? Had it really come from an experienced hacker who could break into systems and see what was there? He had become quite a good one himself, but even he had not been able to bypass the security system, which was based on the Orange Book, standard guidelines for computer security.

Something was coming onto the screen! He followed the instructions carefully, barely understanding what he was doing. It was time to put in the disk with the software he had downloaded.

He continued to follow the instructions, keying in several numbers and symbols. If it was going to work it should be... Some unintelligible signs appeared on the screen, and then the computer suddenly sprang to life. This was what he was waiting for; this was it! He felt himself go hot, and he broke out into a sweat as he saw that he had, indeed, succeeded. He remained for several minutes just staring at the screen. Was this real? This was the answer to all his problems. Or was it really?

A wave of nausea overtook him. This was going to take

him into a different world. Not only would he become rich, but he would become a criminal, a big-time criminal. He would have his feet firmly set on a path he was not quite sure he wanted to go on. He knew that with one success he would not be able to give this up. He poured himself another drink. Perhaps he should do this later. Was he a criminal? Apart from small dishonesties at school, a few lies, and some insignificant underhand business deals as an adult, he had never gone in for something which could be considered a serious crime. Even his hacking activities had been fairly innocuous.

Did he really want it? There was a way back, wasn't there? He could pull out now, start afresh, perhaps leave the company and go to another one, in another town. Where would this take him? But there was Martin to consider, and their weeks and months of planning. Or was it really Martin's planning? He found his mind wandering.

It seemed that ever since he had become a teller, Martin had been looking for someone to work with; someone who would have at least partial access to the computer system; someone who would have sufficient knowledge to "break into" other accounts.

Was it only five months ago that they had spoken? Oh yes, he had known Martin for a long time, but they had never really talked. And then it had been a joke, a joke about how to make "millions."

Though they had not been together often, each time they met they had discussed it more and more, until the joke became a reality. And he sensed that for Martin it had always been a reality.

Their plan was so attractive, so possible, that here he

was now with everything wide open before him. It was going to be so easy.

All Martin had to do was to occasionally type in a few zeros. He would manipulate the records of debits and credits so that everything would balance. And then the world would be theirs.

It had been a struggle to break into the system — until an unexpected break had come when he was surfing the Internet in the privacy of his home. He had gone into news-groups to see what he could find that was new and had stumbled on one dealing with computer security. For many days he had read the postings, learning more about security than he had ever dreamed he would. But no one would give directions as to actually *how* these things were done. How *did* one hack into an account and change the data in order to transfer funds? What he did learn, though, was that in a closed network, if any of the servers or administrators were on the Internet, the security of the system was at risk.

Finally he had posted his own message. He had worded it carefully, asking simply if anyone could assist him in get-ting into a system that a former employee had "locked" in spite. It hadn't sounded suspicious at all.

Eventually he had received a reply from someone who called himself "Jip." The instructions were strange, but he copied them carefully and downloaded the software Jip pro-vided. He had little faith it would work, but it had. Now they could put their plan into action.

But something inside him seemed to revolt. Perhaps he should tell Martin he had not been able to crack the code.

The phone rang. It was the woman from his own bank

phoning him, as she had done regularly for the past few days. Was he going to clear his personal overdraft? It was increasing daily. More of his checks would have to be dishonored.

He pleaded and then begged. She sounded more sympathetic and promised to discuss it with the manager. But she saw little chance he would change his mind. His collateral securities were minimal.

As he put the phone down, a wave of resolve overtook him. They would start their operations immediately!

Martin's voice was breathless. "How did you do it?"

"With some software and some numbers," said the man slowly.

"What software? What numbers? Where did you get them?"

"They were fairly easy to access," he said, suddenly feeling the need to be secretive.

"You must tell me what you did." Martin's voice was commanding.

The man became angry. Who was Martin to speak to him like this?

"I got them from the Internet," he said slowly. "I downloaded them."

"The Internet!" Martin almost shouted. "You sent messages over the Internet? You have left a trail and they will pick us up right away. We can't do anything now. You have ruined things completely!" Martin's voice rose higher and higher in agitation.

"It's quite safe," the man said, cold anger beginning to grip him. "I downloaded some hacking software from a Web site. It only helped because of all the work I had done. On its own it would have been useless."

He realized he could not tell Martin the truth, not about Jip, anyway. He had merely asked an innocent hacking question and people answered them all the time. But Martin wouldn't understand. "All right," Martin said, calming down. "We're on."

Instead of relief, the man felt a pang of conscience, or was it fear? They couldn't be caught. He tried to comfort himself. He had read that corporate America lost billions of dollars annually through illegal access to computer systems. However, most computer theft was not reported, as it might cause a firm's clients to lose faith.

With any luck, this would never be properly followed up. And if it was, internally, there would be dismissal at the worst, but he would have made thousands, tens of thousands, perhaps even millions.

His bank manager would learn to respect him, to see him as one of his most successful clients. His way was clear to him now.

He would start with the Selby firm.

CHAPTER 2

Michael looked out of his office window at the traffic making its way along the Johannesburg streets. The cars looked like the matchbox cars he had played with as a child.

That seemed to be such a long time ago, a time when he had small things to worry about.

His problems had seemed big then, but now he knew what real troubles were.

Sure, everything seemed all right. He had a wife, three lovely children who were quickly growing up, and a baby. He had a good job, a nice home in a sought-after area, and a car.

He was doing well as an accountant at the banking firm in which he worked. He had been in their head office for several years and had come to be liked and respected by the other members of staff. His section was dealing with several major, multimillion rand accounts and had built up a name for efficiency and reliability.

He thought with satisfaction of the handshake he had received only yesterday from one of the senior directors of the bank. James Caldwin had made an unannounced visit, and it was quite a surprise since they had only seen the tall, stately man before in company pictures.

Sally, the receptionist, had paled when relaying the message that Caldwin would be visiting their department within the hour. She had been the first to disappear into the background to survey his dignified face and his swept back, greying hair at a distance. Caldwin had spoken to several members of staff, stopping to shake the hands of Michael and Stephen, saying he had heard of their high-quality work. That should have made Michael feel good, for Caldwin was one of the richest men in Johannesburg and owned immense gold shares.

So what was he worrying about?

Michael was *frum* now. His wife and children were *frum* too, having become *ba'alei teshuvah* three years before.

Their life before seemed to be so long ago, in another lifetime. He had even looked different. His blonde hair had been longer then, much like his older daughter Dina's now. She, too, had hazel eyes and the smattering of freckles around the nose. In fact, even his baby daughter Chanie was following his pattern. But Chanie had not been born then.

They had lived, then, near their present home, and they had everything — everything that all the neighbors had.

But there had been that sense of emptiness.

He had filled the emptiness with dances and discos and cheese-and-wine parties. Until he met Rabbi Sandler. Rabbi Sandler was different from any other rabbi he had known.

Michael had always gone to *shul* on Yom Kippur and Rosh HaShanah, but he had understood little and had climbed back into his car uninspired and somewhat relieved that it was over. His wife, Sandy, had been more involved, but her preparation for the holidays had consisted of frantic shopping for something that would look different and expensive. The biggest tragedy would be if someone arrived in a similar outfit.

Rabbi Sandler had seemed to come from a totally different type of Judaism, though he had reassured them that it was all the same. The whole family had liked the young rabbi immediately. He was frank, open, warm, friendly, and caring. He didn't dress very formally, though he wore a yarmulke and *tzitzis* which stuck out from under his sweater. These had fascinated them all, but they had become used to it.

Their becoming *frum* had increased in a steady way. In fact, at one stage Rabbi Sandler had held them back, waiting till he felt they were "safe" with their present level before they went on to the next one. All in all, it had taken about nine months for them to keep Shabbos, kashrus, *taharas hamishpachah*, and what seemed to be the "big" things in *Yiddishkeit*. It had taken another three months for Sandy to put on a *sheitel*. In one year, they had changed into a "model" newly *frum* family.

The change had been exciting and challenging and, on many levels, frustrating.

It had not been without opposition from family and friends. Sandy's mother had bitterly opposed their moves, bewailing the fact that her home was now not "good enough" for her own children and grandchildren to eat in and that they could no longer drive over on Friday nights. Michael's family had also been antagonistic.

The opposition had raged for around two years, and

then everyone had calmed down and seemed to accept it. The fact that both Michael's and Sandy's parents moved to Cape Town last year made it a whole lot easier. The children — Daniel, Dina, and Sam — had been put into the *mechinah* classes of a Jewish school. As is the way with children, they seemed to adjust within a few months.

Rabbi Sandler had been with them every step of the way, inspiring, guiding, and directing.

Michael sighed as he remembered how close he and the Rabbi had become. He had regarded him as the best friend he ever had. He still was, in a way, but he could no longer really talk to him. He couldn't work out how this had come about. The Rabbi's caring seemed to have cooled down. He was interested in other families, interested in making other people *frum*. He didn't seem to have the same kind of time for them anymore. Michael felt a certain bitterness creep over him.

"People make you *frum* and then they just desert you!" Maybe it wasn't worth it after all. He turned angrily away from the window and went to sit at his desk, poring over the figures he was working on, the resentment still pervading his entire being.

It wasn't that he didn't want to be *frum*. Why did he feel rejected and pushed aside? His feelings of confusion were replaced by a further rush of resentment. Were they no longer good enough or important or clever enough for the Rabbi? He looked at the screen in front of him. He had work to do. He mustn't get bogged down by these thoughts.

He worked for several minutes in the quiet office. The secretaries had already left, as had most of the other staff. He needed to look at these figures before he left the office. It shouldn't take long, not long at all.

Suddenly he drew his breath in sharply. These figures didn't add up. There was something wrong. Resentment was replaced by uneasiness and a funny crawling feeling inside his stomach. Large amounts of money from the Selby Construction Company account were not accounted for. Something appeared to be drastically wrong. He checked and rechecked.

"Hey, Michael," said a voice, and he looked up to see his colleague, Stephen, looking at him in concern.

"Michael, it's time to go. They've already shut down the switchboard. What's wrong, Michael?"

Michael switched off the computer terminal and gave a sigh.

"Just a small problem," he said. "I'll look at it again tomorrow."

He looked at his watch.

Yes, it was late. He should have left fifteen minutes ago.

He had to be in time for *minchah*. He couldn't let the minyan down...again.

CHAPTER 3

Sandy changed the baby's diaper for maybe the tenth time that day. Something was wrong. The baby was listless and she seemed feverish. Well, if she wasn't better by the next day, Sandy would call the doctor. She was probably just teething.

Daniel burst into the room, wrinkled up his nose, and walked out quickly. He was a slightly overweight young man of twelve years (baby fat, people said) with sea blue eyes and straight, pitch-black hair.

"I would like to speak to you, Ma, but in a few minutes."

She settled the baby and went into Daniel's room to see what her eldest son needed.

"Could you help me at all with my homework?" he asked. "I really can't make head or tail of it, and I don't know who to ask."

She picked up the book, hoping it was history or math or biology. She had done well in those subjects at school. It was *Chumash* with *Rashi*, and she felt a wave of inadequacy sweep over her.

She had learned to read Hebrew fairly well in the last

three years, but *Chumash* with *Rashi* was difficult. There was the English translation, but Daniel said he had already looked there.

Sandy smiled. Even Daniel had realized that in Jewish studies the children were far outstripping their parents in knowledge, and he began to patiently explain his question and what Rashi said and then the answer.

"You see," he said gaily, "it did help to ask you. When you have to explain to someone who is unlearned, then the inspiration comes."

Unlearned! she thought. Here she was with a degree cum laude from one of the best universities, and her son was calling her unlearned. But she had to admit that, though she already knew much more than the average woman of her age about *Yiddishkeit*, she had only begun to "nibble" the edge of all there was to know.

Sandy had been happy to become *frum*. Life had taken on a very new and definite meaning when seen in the Jewish context.

She saw her face framed by a purple and a blue monster which was stuck onto the mirror. It was an attractive, sensitive face with dark curls and blue eyes. She was, of course, wearing a *sheitel*, but this resembled her own hair almost exactly and was in the style she had always worn. Except, of course, the *sheitel* looked better somehow.

She had also felt she could speak to Rabbi Sandler and his wife, Sara. They had been, and still were, extremely good friends.

She was aware that her husband had lost some of his enthusiasm for *Yiddishkeit*, and this worried her. He had been the driving force behind the changes they had made, and he had persevered against all odds, but now he seemed tired.

She walked into Sam and Dina's room and immediately gave a groan. They had been painting and on the carpet was a large, blue stain.

"I'm sorry, Mommy," said Sam, looking up with round, innocent blue eyes that matched a paint spot lodged on his nose. A streak of red paint colored his hair and there was a dab of yellow on his chin. Dina was in no better shape. Her neck was covered in a mixture of blue and red which made gruesome purple marks where the two merged. She also looked as if she had given herself a black eye. Her hands were a rainbow of colors with occasional muddy patches.

"We'll wipe it up. Really we will. But don't you like our painting?" Sam held up what probably would have made a fortune in a modern art display, but seemed to have no meaning at all. The paint was still wet, and it brushed against the corner of the duvet and then onto his yarmulke.

"Couldn't you have used newspaper?" Sandy asked.

"Yes, but you wouldn't get such a good painting. The print would be in the way," said Dina.

"No," Sandy said. "I mean newspaper to cover the floors. Couldn't you have used that?"

"We could have," Dina said philosophically, "but we started painting and we just never had time to look for it."

Sandy brought them a rag to mop up the floor and gathered up the rug to send to the cleaners, then she went to make supper. Michael would be home soon and he always wanted her to have the meal ready, just as his mother had done, she thought with a sigh.

She remembered the early years of their marriage when he had constantly compared his mother's cooking to her somewhat elementary attempts. She had been angry with him then, very angry, and had been angry with his mother, too. Then he had always wanted to go and eat in his mother's house, at least twice a week if not more.

But even before they had become kosher, he had gradually stopped eating at his Mom's and even needed persuasion to go and see his parents occasionally. Now there were mostly just phone calls and faxes.

Her thoughts were interrupted by the ring of the front doorbell. Her hands were wet from the salad, and she waited for someone to answer.

The bell rang again. Still no response from the rest of the household.

"Sam!" she called. "Sam, please open the door."

"What did you say, Mommy?" shouted Sam.

"The door, Sam, the door...or Dina...oh dear..." she said as the bell rang again. "I suppose I'll have to answer it myself." Quickly she dried her hands on a towel and went to the hallway.

The bell was pushed harder this time.

"I'm sorry," she said as she opened it. "I thought someone else was going to answer."

Standing there was Richard, the boy from next door. He wanted to see Daniel. She frowned. What was it about Richard that made her feel so uneasy? He was always polite and quiet. Was it the way he looked? He was fairly tall for his age, and had mousy brown hair which was always a little untidy and looked as if it insisted on going in directions of its own. Perhaps his eyes made her uneasy. They were often red and bloodshot or even glassy. Obviously he had some allergy problems — in fact, he had even mentioned this. But it wasn't that.

Still feeling uneasy, she let him in and he walked into Daniel's room, shutting the door behind him. Why didn't she want him to be with Daniel?

Richard was Jewish, though not even remotely *frum*. He was two-and-a-half years older than Daniel, but that wasn't the problem. There was something about him, something about the way he looked at her, that made her feel he was years and years older than Daniel, and that he wasn't quite honest. But there was nothing at all to confirm this.

What could she say? She didn't want to be the kind of mother who would only let her children play with *frum* or even Jewish children. She wasn't going to separate them from the rest of the world. *Yiddishkeit*, yes, that was very important to the family, but not to go overboard! And what did she really have against Richard? He hadn't had much of a chance in life. His parents had been on the verge of divorce for at least five years and were more or less leading divided lives, leaving Richard and his sister Tanya very much to themselves.

Richard's father had also been drinking heavily. What chance did the boy have?

But their house was nice. They had a pool, and a sauna, and Daniel loved to go there. Swimming was good for him. How could she stop him?

A key turned in the lock. Michael was arriving home and

supper was not yet ready. As he entered she saw the bitter expression which had only recently appeared around his mouth. He also looked anxious, but she had learned to wait until he confided his worries to her. He always did, usually late at night when the rest of the household was asleep.

"I won't be long, Michael," she said as she rushed to the kitchen to check if the potatoes were at last becoming soft. She sighed as she saw that the food was not yet edible. She would really have to get a microwave one day, so that she could produce supper in minutes rather than hours.

"Michael, are you feeling well?" she asked as he followed her into the kitchen. "You're looking awfully pale."

"I'm well," he said. "*Baruch Hashem*." He offered no further comment.

"How was *shul*?" she asked. "Who was there?"

"Oh, the Rav, and the usual people. We actually had eleven today so I didn't really have to go."

"But you wanted to go, didn't you?" She remembered the days when Michael would put everything aside for that minyan.

"Oh, I suppose I wanted to," he said. "I mean, I can't let the minyan down. It's just that it isn't the same way it was. No one seems really enthusiastic anymore."

"Maybe it will get better," she said hopefully. She took the lid off the pot and saw the undercooked potatoes. "I'm sorry, but I've been very busy with Chanie. I have to keep changing her diaper. I gave her a bit of ground rice in the bottle so maybe it will get better, otherwise I'll have to call the doctor."

Michael left the kitchen to see the baby and returned almost immediately. "She needs a new diaper," he said, picking up a newspaper and going towards the living room. "She looks quite cheerful, though. She gurgled very happily when she saw me."

Sandy sighed. She would have to buy some more diapers. How could a child go through so many in one afternoon?

CHAPTER 4

Sandy dragged herself out of bed for the fifteenth time that night. The baby was extremely restless, and hot, and seemed to be sleeping very little. Her crying was incessant and nothing seemed to satisfy her. She would have to see the doctor in the morning.

She stumbled over to the crib, wondering why on earth she had had another baby, and was immediately smitten by a pang of guilt.

She really did love her. She wouldn't exchange her for anything, and yet, tonight, Chanie woke her up every time she closed her eyes, and she was just exhausted. The night before had also been bad — but not like this.

The diaper was dirty again and Sandy changed it, trying to soothe the baby. She settled her down and Chanie appeared to be sleeping. For how long? Not very long at all, she was sure.

She dragged herself back to bed, pulling the blankets over her. She was so tired that she had expected to fall asleep almost immediately, but sleep wouldn't come. Anxiety came instead, one worry after another.

Michael hadn't confided in her. He had been unusually quiet that night, and when she had tried to find out what was wrong, he had shut up like a clam. What could be worrying him? Was it his work? Was it the Rabbi?

Sandy awoke with a start as the early morning sun streamed in through the bedroom window. The baby was crying again, pitifully. How long had she been crying? How long had she been asleep? No one else was awake.

She looked at her watch.

Five-ten A.M. She would have to wake up Michael so that he could daven and put on *tefillin* before he went to work. Perhaps he would even catch the early morning minyan. But that was not likely. He hadn't been to that minyan for several months now. It had been difficult in winter for him to get to work on time, but now it was summer and he still found it difficult. He always said he would start going to the minyan again soon, but he never got around to it.

She went to the baby, changing her once again and feeling guilty at how red and sore she looked. She really must call the doctor, but it was not an emergency. She'd wait till seven o'clock, though there was no way she could go back to sleep now.

She settled the baby again and went to the kitchen to make some coffee. As she boiled the kettle she said the morning *berachos*. She supposed she shouldn't really be doing that. She had always said *berachos* with a great deal of concentration, and then, when the baby was born, she had started saying them while she was doing other things. After all, she could have stopped saying *berachos* altogether if she didn't have time.

She was not in a hurry at the moment. In fact, she had a lot of time on her hands — but habit ruled and she finished her *berachos*, not being really sure if she had said them all or not. She would fix that sometime, somehow. Anyway, women didn't really have to daven, did they?

She drank her coffee and cut herself a slice of cake. She shouldn't be eating cake. But she was tired and she was sure she needed sugar for quick energy.

The baby started to cry, and she banged down the cup as a wave of irritation swept over her. Not again! Not again! Surely she could give her some peace for half an hour at least. She walked into Chanie's room, still irritated. The baby seemed to sense her mood. She stopped crying and looked at her for a few seconds, and then her face contorted as she began to cry again. Sandy changed her again and tried to give her water, but the baby only sucked for a few seconds and then gave up.

Sandy was worried. Chanie didn't look well at all. She wasn't drinking well, and she was hot. Sandy was afraid she might become dehydrated — she had better call the doctor soon.

She heard Michael's alarm clock bleeping on and on, and then the sound stopped suddenly. Michael had switched it off.

She waited for a few minutes and then went into the bedroom to speak to him. He had fallen asleep again, his hand still clasping the alarm clock.

He gave a groan as she woke him up. "Not already," he said. "I was kept up all night. That baby!"

Indignation rushed over her. "I was the one who was up

with the baby all night! I didn't even know you were awake! It would have been nice for you to keep me company while I took care of *your* baby!"

At seven o'clock she called the doctor. He would include their home on his morning rounds. Possibly in an hour, an hour and a half.... It wasn't urgent, was it? Not really.

Now there were the other children to attend to, to get ready for school.

The school bus would soon be at the door. They were never quite ready to catch it. There was always a little extra honking from the bus driver every morning. It was as though each child would work out his time with precisely this in mind: to leave everything till the last two minutes and be almost, but not quite, ready.

Dina couldn't find her other shoe. Who had taken it? Where was it? How could she go to school with only one shoe?

Honking was heard outside, a final scramble, shoe found, rush and shouting, and then sudden quiet.

Michael had already gone to work. He usually waited until the children had gone. Perhaps there was something worrying him at the office.

The baby had been very quiet — at least she had finally settled down. Perhaps she was getting better. Perhaps she needn't have called the doctor. She could have just taken her to the doctor's office in the afternoon.

She tiptoed into the room and looked toward the crib. The baby was very still, and her skin was a strange greyish red.

Sandy's heart gave a jump. Had something terrible happened to the baby? She heard a tiny whimper and she felt a flood of relief overwhelming her.

The doorbell rang, and she quickly let the doctor in. He could see that she was badly shocked, and he went straight into the baby's room. He looked at the baby for only a few seconds and asked to use the telephone.

"I am sending her to hospital," he said. "You must go there immediately. She needs to be on a drip and she needs urgent attention."

Sandy opened her mouth to speak but no words came out.

"In fact," he said, "I will inform them by phone and join you there later."

She started to pack some things for the baby, but he almost pushed her out of the door, and before she realized it she was driving up to the hospital entrance.

She carried the baby into reception, and the receptionist waved her on towards the children's ward.

"Doctor phoned already," she said. "He said it was urgent. The nurse is waiting for you."

She carried the limp baby and was relieved to place her in the nurse's hands. Her skin felt dry and hot, her eyes looked sunken. She didn't even look like Chanie. She looked distorted and strange.

Sandy sank into a chair in the waiting room, picking up a magazine. She could only flip through the pictures...and she was so tired.

CHAPTER 5

He's early today, I wonder what's wrong," Sally said. The receptionist looked suspiciously at Michael as he walked down the passage towards his office. Her mouth was set in a grim line.

"Why should anything be wrong?" asked Michelle, an attractive young woman whose large green eyes seemed almost permanently to hold a look of surprise.

"Well, Mr. Berman is never early. I have been here for many years, long before he came, and I have never known him to be early."

Her voice trailed off as her supervisor walked into the office, and she immediately busied herself with the computer, striking a figure of intense efficiency. After all, the distinguished Mr. Caldwin, only two days ago, had congratulated them on their efficiency and their good service to the bank. How could she not work hard? Michelle continued to paint her nails, waiting till they were dry before she attacked the keyboard.

Michael, meanwhile, had gone into his office and switched on the terminal. Those figures had to be wrong.

There had to be some answer, somewhere. Was there something wrong with the program? He checked into the other accounts. These seemed to be in order. He went back to the Selby figures. He had to find out what had gone wrong.

Sandy put down the magazine and started to pace up and down the waiting room. She saw the doctor arrive, nod to her, and go towards the children's section. She wanted to rush after him and ask him what was happening, but she stopped herself. He needed to be with the baby, her baby. What was happening to her baby? A wave of helplessness swept over her...and loneliness.

"Please, could I use the phone?" she asked the receptionist. Very soon she was talking to Sara Sandler. She would be at the hospital right away.

That would help. It would help a lot!

She thought she had better phone Michael. She didn't want to worry him too much. She just told him that the baby had been taken to the hospital to be put on a drip. Dehydration.... No, not to worry.

Yet she knew instinctively that the baby was dangerously ill. Maybe... Heaven forbid! But she had wanted to protect Michael from more anxiety. What was he so worried about? She still didn't know.

She picked up the magazine again and flicked over the pages. She couldn't concentrate on anything. What did one do in this situation? Daven? Say *tehillim*? Anyway, Sara Sandler would soon arrive. She would know what to do.

What was wrong with the baby? Would she be all right? Why had everyone looked so worried, almost grave? Was it her fault? Had she called the doctor too late? Surely the baby would not... Heaven forbid... Surely nothing would happen to the baby. How could they live without little Chanie?

She felt her fear building up inside of herself and felt dizzy and sick.

How did doctors tell parents when their children had died? What did they say?

She began to imagine all kinds of scenes. The doors to the children's section would swing open, the doctor would come out to her with a very serious expression on his face, and he would say: "I am sorry, Mrs. Berman, I am afraid...."

It was too horrible to think of. Her thoughts were racing.

"I am sorry, Mrs. Berman, I am afraid..." The doctor had come out through the swing doors and was facing her. He was saying those words. Her heart pounded, and she felt she was going to faint.

"Are you all right, Mrs. Berman?" he was saying. "Could someone get you some water?" He looked at her with concern.

"My baby," she said. "She, she is..."

"She is very ill," he said, and she felt an immediate flood of relief. "I think we probably caught it in time, but I am afraid she will have to stay in the hospital for several days."

She started to cry with relief.

"Would you like to go and see her now?" he asked. "Don't be anxious about the drips, we have to do this. She needs a lot of fluid and electrolytes."

She followed the doctor into the ward, still feeling weak and shaky.

Chanie was lying in a large steel crib with tubes coming out of her head. She looked like a stranger.

A wave of fear swept over Sandy.

"Will she really be all right?" she asked.

"We hope so," answered the doctor. "We always hope for the best."

She called to the child, but there was no response. She felt herself becoming faint. A nurse held on to her arm.

"Mrs. Berman, you are looking very pale. Perhaps you should come and sit down. We will look after Chanie."

She led her to a waiting room, and she sat in a chair and picked up another magazine. She felt tired and very, very weak. What was going to happen? Would Chanie be okay? She heard someone come into the room and saw Sara Sandler walking towards her, her dark eyes showing concern.

She immediately burst into tears and started to sob. "Chanie is very, very ill, and I am sure it is my fault, and maybe she will die, and...."

Sara put her arms around her and let her cry.

The sobbing grew quiet and then stopped.

"What is happening with Chanie?" Sara asked, gently handing her friend some more tissues.

"She is dehydrated, and the doctor said she is very, very ill... and she has drips all over her head, and she doesn't look like Chanie anymore."

Sandy started to sob again, and Sara pulled out a small book from her bag and started to say *tehillim*.

"Where is Hashem when these things happen?" Sandy asked.

"Right here, where He always is," Sara said. "Our

awareness of Him might sometimes get dimmer because of something happening within ourselves, but He never goes away or becomes more distant."

Sandy said nothing and Sara carried on with the *tehillim*. The words had a soothing effect on Sandy. At least something was being done.

Time went by....

"Hello, how's the baby?" She looked up to see Rabbi Sandler in the room.

"I got Sara's note saying where she had gone, and I came over right away to see how you all were. How is Michael taking it?"

"He doesn't really know it is so serious," Sandy said. "I didn't want to worry him. He has so many things to worry about."

"What things?" asked the Rabbi.

Sandy blushed. She didn't really want to explain that Rabbi Sandler was probably a large part of the problem.

Rabbi Sandler was, however, extremely sensitive to the feelings of others and, as he caught her expression, he made a mental note to speak to Michael, at length.

CHAPTER 6

S tephen stood behind Michael's terminal and watched him for a few seconds. Michael swung around quickly and looked almost guilty.

"Is there anything the matter, Michael?" Stephen asked.

"No, no," Michael said. "Why do you ask?"

"Well, you seem to be very edgy."

"My baby is sick," said Michael shortly. "I was kept awake all night."

"I'm sorry," Stephen said. "Is she better now?"

Michael didn't answer, and Stephen walked away. Michael did not seem to be himself. Even the secretary had mentioned it that morning.

Michael looked at the figures again, hoping somehow, somewhere, there had been a mistake. How could so much money simply be missing?

Perhaps by a little maneuvering and working backwards, he might be able to see exactly what had happened. He typed in some figures. Now it appeared as if the "mistake" had been accounted for, and to do that had been so easy. And now to investigate. He would erase all these false figures, but he just wanted to see what it would look like.

The telephone rang. He picked it up. Sandy was on the line. She was saying that he should come to the hospital right away — the baby had taken a turn for the worse. The Sandlers had been there for some time.

"Little Chanie," he stammered as he quickly packed his things, everything else flying out of his mind, and within minutes he had explained to his colleagues what was happening and was rushing towards his car.

His thoughts were racing. Would Chanie live? Sandy had sounded very, very serious. Surely Chanie would live. Surely she couldn't die. Surely Hashem wouldn't let that happen.

His hands were trembling so much that he found difficulty fitting the key into the ignition. He tried to start the car several times before he realized that the security lock was still activated. He drove to the hospital at high speed, as if in a dream, a sense of foreboding overwhelming him. Why? Oh why?

Everything had been fine only yesterday. He hadn't had worries then, not terrible ones like these. In fact, no worry could compare with what he was feeling now — fearing for the life of his daughter. Everything else just faded into the background.

As he walked into the hospital, he was met at the door by Rabbi Sandler, who was holding a *sefer Tehillim*. How had he gotten there so quickly? Perhaps he did care still, a little.

"How is she?" he asked.

"She wasn't doing too badly," said the Rabbi. "And then she suddenly took a turn for the worse. They are waiting for you."

Michael followed him into the ward, a cold, icy fear settling into his chest. Would Chanie be all right?

He looked at Chanie. She was a very strange color and her skin looked different. They had had to shave off some of her hair, and there were so many tubes coming out of her head. That wasn't Chanie. That couldn't be Chanie. It didn't look like Chanie at all. There must be some mistake.

He saw Sandy and Sara, white-faced, both saying *tehillim*.

"What can I do?" he asked.

Rabbi Sandler silently handed him a *sefer Tehillim* book. He started to say *tehillim*, but found that the words were becoming blurred and the paper damp. He continued, turning over one page after another. An hour went by, two hours.

Sandy felt faint, and Rabbi and Mrs. Sandler took her out to the waiting room, but Michael found that he could not move. He felt rooted to the spot, unable to do anything except say *tehillim*. They didn't deserve this; surely they didn't deserve this. How could Hashem be doing this to them?

A picture of Chanie at her six-month birthday party forced its way into his mind. She was dressed in a powder-blue velvet dress which she kept stroking because she loved the feel of it. Sandy had brushed her soft, wispy hair and tied it with a shiny blue ribbon. The Rabbi's younger children were there, and Shevi and Zevi had helped organize games. There had been several newly *frum* mothers with their babies and small children. He had felt good, then, really good. He had been happy with his family, happy with his community.

His mind went further back to the time Chanie was born. There had been such excitement, and the Sandlers had been there shortly afterwards to bring Sandy food and to see the new baby. Sara had looked after Sandy throughout her stay in the hospital and beyond. They had been so caring, so.... Other pictures came and went: Chanie laughing at a new toy, or playing in the sandpit with her soft hair covered in sand, trying to taste everything she found. Chanie was a treasure from Hashem. They would never have dreamed of having more children if they hadn't become *frum*. He couldn't really imagine not being *frum*; but it wasn't the same as it used to be. Something had been lost along the way. Whose fault was it? Could he do something about it? He would have to.

But now only Chanie was important, and saying *tehillim* for her. They couldn't, Heaven forbid, lose Chanie. She had to be well. Everything inside of him ached with a longing to see her smile. Time went on and on. He did not even look at the crib. He just couldn't bear to see Chanie that way.

Finally, he glanced up. Yes, it was Chanie, and she was beginning to look more like Chanie. Her color was more like the color a baby's skin should be. She was looking more like a baby, not like something foreign and distorted. Could she be getting better?

At that moment the doctor walked in, went over to the baby, and then turned to Michael.

"She's going to make it," he said, smiling.

The *sefer Tehillim* immediately became soaking wet.

As Michael returned to his office, he felt an odd combination of exhilaration and anxiety. He felt as if he had been taken on an emotional roller coaster which had threatened to eject him at any moment.

Though he had only been absent for about four hours, he felt as if he had been away for days, that he was returning from another world.

However, he was quickly jerked back into a terrifying reality.

"Oh, thank goodness you're here," Stephen said. "We actually thought you would be much longer. The firm urgently needed those figures you were working on, and you weren't here to give them, but I looked and saw that you had just about completed everything, so I did the finishing touches and gave them a printout."

For the second time that day it felt as if an icy hand was clutching at Michael's heart. He opened his mouth to say something but no sound came out.

"Are you all right?" Stephen asked.

"Yes, yes," he said. "It's just that my baby nearly died. She's okay now."

"I think you should go home and come back tomorrow," Stephen said. "We can manage. You are beginning to look like a ghost."

CHAPTER 7

It was Sunday afternoon three weeks later. Chanie had improved rapidly, and was now very much her "old self." Michael and Sandy had deeply appreciated how the Sandlers had been with them, and their feelings had warmed towards their mentors and towards *Yiddishkeit* in general.

Michael had not done anything about the missing money. He had planned to do something the following day, but he hadn't really known what to say and had put it off for the next day, and then the next, until it became increasingly difficult. Nothing seemed to be happening, so for the time being, he just let things ride. He hadn't done anything wrong. He hadn't taken any money. But someone had. Who?

Things at the office were relatively quiet, and in general, life had returned to normal.

The telephone rang. Michael heard Sandy going to answer it.

"Are you sure you're okay, Grandpa?" she was saying. "What does your doctor say? Are you sure you can look after yourself? Please, just hold on."

He heard her footsteps coming towards him.

"Michael," she said, and her voice had a tremor. "Michael, Grandpa has had a slight stroke. He says he is fine and can look after himself, and he really sounds all right, but I'm worried." She looked at him questioningly.

"Can't he come and stay with us for a few weeks?" Michael asked, knowing that was what Sandy was really asking.

She looked relieved.

It was then arranged that Grandpa would stay with them. He would come within the next few days, as soon as he could organize his affairs.

The children were delighted.

Mommy's Grandpa (he refused categorically to be called Zadie) lived for many years in America, and though they kept close contact with him by phone and fax, to have him stay for a prolonged visit was, indeed, exciting.

He had been left a widower many years before and had always cherished his independence. The fact that he had agreed to come and stay with them so readily meant that he himself was becoming anxious about his health.

"Exactly how old is your Grandpa?" Daniel asked.

Sandy frowned. "Well," she said, "he must be at least ninety, *k'naina hara*, and he has been the picture of health all this time."

"That's very old," said Sam. "Maybe he'll be one hundred soon, and that's very, very old. That's antique."

"*K'naina hara*," Sandy said again.

And so it was that within a few days, Grandpa had come to stay. He had always been a very proud, health-conscious, trim man who carried himself in a way that caused many people to stop and look at him. He had been a master of the business world and had made and lost several fortunes, retiring fairly comfortably.

He was still a very striking figure, despite slight weakness on the right side and a barely perceptible limp, produced by the recent stroke. His thinning hair was a milky white, and his piercing blue eyes denoted an awareness and sensitivity to everything around him. He had brought many books with him, having been for much of his life a devoted follower of "good" English literature. He had also brought his cellular phone.

His delight at seeing the children was immeasurable. They, in turn, had been extremely pleased to see him and to open the many interesting presents he had brought them.

"I didn't bring them any candy," he told Sandy. "Your mother has informed me that nothing is kosher enough for your family, so I wasn't going to risk it. Anyway, candy is bad for their teeth, their cholesterol, and it is fattening!"

On the second day after Grandpa arrived, Richard came over to see Daniel. He greeted the adults as he walked to Daniel's room, closing the door behind him as always.

"Who is that?" Grandpa asked.

"That's Richard, the boy from next door," Sandy said. Surely Grandpa would not disapprove. Grandpa didn't even pretend to be "*frum.*"

"The boy is on drugs," Grandpa said. "You can tell by his eyes."

"But...but are you sure?" she asked, bewildered. How could Grandpa know?

"I have seen enough of it," said Grandpa. "Where I live there is far too much of it, and you can tell a mile away who is taking drugs and who isn't. That Richard definitely is. Shall I speak to him?"

Sandy was horrified. "No, Grandpa, please don't. What if you are wrong?"

"But Sandy, you don't want Daniel to take drugs, do you? It isn't good for him. Richard is sure to give him some. You have to be careful with whom your children associate these days. Peer pressure is so strong."

Sandy's heart turned a double somersault. Daniel. Drugs. She felt faint.

It must be Grandpa's imagination. He was very old, after all. What would he know about drugs? She hoped Grandpa wouldn't embarrass Richard.

However, the moment Richard came out of Daniel's room, Grandpa indicated that he would like a word with him in the garden outside. Richard faced Grandpa with an attitude of embarrassment, defiance, and curiosity. What did this old man want from him?

As soon as they had walked to the far side of the garden, Grandpa came quickly to the point. "You are smoking marijuana," he said to Richard, his eyes fixing the boy.

Richard, about to deny it, thought better of it. "I suppose so," he said.

"I don't want you smoking around my great-grandson," Grandpa said flatly.

"Oh, but I don't," said Richard. "I really don't. I wouldn't do that. I only do it at home when no one is there, in the garden, really."

"Your parents don't know?"

"No, no, I'm sure they don't. And if they did...well...I'm not sure if they would say anything."

"Of course they would say something," Grandpa said, his eyes blazing.

Richard gave a sigh. "In some ways, I wish they would. But they are busy, really busy."

"Are they both working?"

"My father works, of course, and my mother doesn't, but she is always busy with...she is busy doing...whatever she is doing. They don't really put restrictions on us."

"That makes you lucky?"

"Well, my friends say that, but it doesn't make me feel so great. Some of the guys I know, they have to tell their parents where they are going and what time they'll be back, and they sometimes have a curfew. They moan about it, but I envy them because at least they know someone is looking out for them."

"And your parents don't care?"

"Oh, I suppose they care, but they are busy with their own lives. They are always fighting, and my father drinks, and that hurts a lot because I love them both. Smoking this stuff makes me feel better, not so alone or so tense."

"But it's not good for you," Grandpa said.

"There isn't any proof of that, is there?"

"There is more and more proof coming out," said Grandpa. "I had to find out about it because some of the people working for me started using it. Their quality of work went down on every level, and they weren't even aware of it. When I forced them to become aware of it, it didn't seem like they really cared. It seemed to do something to their judgment and their ability to think logically. They lost their enjoyment in living, and their eyes became red and they had this look of apathy and indifference in them."

Richard instinctively put his hand over his eyes.

"How's your schoolwork going, my boy?"

Richard was silent. What right had this man to ask him these questions? Yet he found he could not be resentful for long in the face of such obvious sincerity.

"It's always been up and down. I don't study much now. I don't remember what I'm learning anyway, and I don't have the patience to sit in front of my books all day. I actually do well, sometimes, but now I feel it isn't worth all the effort. I just have to pass each term."

"And you're sure you're not influencing Daniel in this direction?"

"No, I wouldn't do that. But I don't think it's a problem that I smoke. It's not dangerous or anything."

Grandpa gave Richard a somber look. "It can cause huge problems when you are married and want to have children yourself," he said. "It can damage your lungs and liver and even your brain. Your whole immune system is being compromised."

Richard frowned. "That can't be true. People don't put themselves at risk like that."

"Look it up yourself, son," Grandpa said. "Do your own research. Do you go to libraries?"

"I used to."

"Think about it. And I don't want to see you around here until you're cleaned up," said Grandpa sternly.

Richard's eyes opened wide. "Not come here? But I love coming here. You don't know what my home is like. I can't relax at all when my parents are home. My father gets violent and starts breaking things and shouting and swearing and carrying on. Coming here is like an oasis in a desert. The Bermans are so different. They have a way of looking at life as if it really has meaning."

"You are Jewish, aren't you Richard?"

"Yes, of course I am. I'm even a *kohen*. But I never really go to *shul* except for a bar mitzvah or wedding."

"Maybe you should become *frum*," Grandpa said seriously.

Richard looked at Grandpa, staring very pointedly at his bare head. "You aren't *frum*," he said.

"Oh, I am a little bit," said Grandpa. "I'm getting more and more every day, hanging around this family of mine."

"But I couldn't be religious," Richard said. "My family doesn't keep any of the laws."

"You want to do everything your family does?"

"Oh no! I want to be absolutely different from them. Not that I don't love them," Richard added quickly, "but I don't want to do what they are doing, especially my father."

"Do you know the rabbi that my family goes to?" Grandpa asked.

"Rabbi Sandler? I know of him but I've never met him."

"Maybe you should. Maybe you should have a chat with him."

Richard faced Grandpa squarely. "Why are you telling me all this? Why don't you just tell me to keep away?"

"I am telling you to keep away, for a while at least. You

are certainly not irreversibly addicted. After a few bad nights and edgy days, you'll be able to leave the drugs behind for good."

The boy looked suddenly incredibly vulnerable. "Please, could I ask you something?"

"Go ahead," said Grandpa. He was beginning to like Richard.

"Do you really care? I mean, does it mean anything to you if I stop smoking the stuff?"

"I do and it does," Grandpa said emphatically.

"But I'm just the boy from next door who you want to get rid of because you don't want Daniel corrupted. Shouldn't I just disappear?"

"Why are you angry with me, son?" Grandpa looked at Richard sadly.

Richard sighed. "I am not really. Just a little bit, and I was far more angry a few minutes ago."

"Well, Richard, you have a choice. You can be angry and full of self-pity. You can hate me and hate all of us, but believe me, as the saying goes, 'Anger and hate do far more harm to the vessel in which they are stored than the vessel over which they are poured.' You will only be harming yourself if you withdraw into anger and resentment, and I would be very disappointed."

Richard looked at the ground. "I'm sorry," he said. "It's just that it is so easy to give up and fall into bad habits."

"The choice is yours," said Grandpa. He shook Richard's hand and headed back into the house.

Richard closed the gate behind him and looked back to check that no one had seen him. He knew his face was a burning red, and he did not want to meet anyone. What would the rest of the family say if they knew about Grandpa's little chat? Surely they had seen through the windows. He walked towards his house and then continued past. He didn't feel like going home just now. His mother would notice that he was upset and start asking him questions, and that was the last thing he wanted. As he walked, he found himself becoming more and more angry. How dare that old man speak to him like that. Who was he, anyway? He wasn't *his* grandfather.

But why had he spoken to him? Why should he be concerned and why should he care? He didn't know him at all. The old man was only concerned because he didn't want Richard to be a bad influence on his family. He had pretended to care just to get him off the premises.

He began to feel more and more bitter. He had liked the Bermans. He had enjoyed being in their house. It was the only house he felt he could relax in. As he had explained to their Grandpa, he had never smoked marijuana in their home. He had never, in their home, done anything even closely connected with it. He hadn't even smoked a cigarette there. He had been straight with his friend and told him about it, but in no way had he ever tried to influence him. In fact, if any of the Bermans had even looked at drugs in any form, he would have been the first to stop them. It was a bad scene. He knew that himself.

Grandpa had offered him a strange alternative: to speak to the Rabbi, to become religious, and to clean up his life on every level. It sounded good in a way, but it could never happen, not to him. His was a different kind of family. His father was an alcoholic. That wasn't much better than drugs. It was just that drugs were illegal and alcohol wasn't. He was doing very much what his father was doing, escaping from a very difficult situation. But then, his difficult situation was his father's drinking and his parents constant fighting. His father said he was drinking to escape from his wife's nagging; but the nagging was mainly due to the drinking, wasn't it? Richard quickened his pace. Walking always helped him think.

Why did Grandpa want him to be religious? Grandpa wasn't even religious himself. He had gathered that from the Berman family and from Grandpa himself. He pictured himself wearing a yarmulke, learning some kind of Jewish book. He would have to keep Shabbos, to keep kosher. But why had Grandpa not suggested that he just take on a few things, that he try to eat kosher meat and to keep a little bit of Shabbos?

Suddenly he understood. If he did it slowly and painlessly there would hardly be any challenge. Perhaps Grandpa had realized that he was a person who could only respond to a challenge. But did he want to give up smoking marijuana? Did he want to become religious, totally religious? He would have to change his whole life. His schoolmates would think he had gone crazy. He let out a sigh which seemed to come from deep inside him. How was he to choose? He suddenly realized that his feet had chosen for him. Here he was, right at the Rabbi's house, and he could see that Rabbi Sandler was home.

In the meanwhile, Sandy had reluctantly informed Daniel what Grandpa's suspicions were.

"He's right, Ma," said Daniel, causing his mother's heart to sink. "I know all about that, he told me a long time ago."

"But you, Daniel. How can you associate with him?"

"Well," said Daniel, "he lives next door and he is good company, and you never seemed to mind. And I wouldn't take drugs — that's not my style."

"Well," she said. "That's that. He is too close by. We'll have to move."

"Ma," said Daniel. "I am not going to take drugs. I wouldn't do that, and he has never tried to get me to take drugs, honest. Please don't send him away or look for another place to live."

Neither, in fact, were necessary, for after Grandpa's talk, Richard avoided Daniel and was not seen by the family for several weeks.

CHAPTER 8

They were at the airport, waiting for a southbound plane... There was excitement everywhere. A boarding announcement was made. They were late, they had to hurry.

Where were they supposed to go? They searched frantically for the right entrance, but a man blocked their way.

Michael tried to reason with him, and then began to shout.

"What are you doing? I have to catch my plane.... Get out of my way... Hey.... HEY...."

Michael blinked and shook his head. He was daydreaming. He stared at his *tefillin* wrapped around his arm and then at his Siddur. He had covered several pages of the *Amidah*, saying the words and going through the motions while dreaming about the man blocking his way at the airport. He started guiltily and carried on davening. He would concentrate — really get into the davening.

What had Stephen said yesterday? He wanted some papers found. What were those papers? Where were they?

He finished davening, realizing that he had not been

able to concentrate. This had been happening to him too often lately. Was it really that important? A man had to daven three times a day, but sometimes it took up such a lot of time and he hardly paid attention to the words.

He remembered when he had first become *frum*. Davening had been exciting then, even though he had to break his teeth over the words. His Hebrew reading had been very rusty — not used since his bar mitzvah. Rabbi Sandler had encouraged him and guided him. Where was he now? Michael still needed encouragement and help and guidance, but Rabbi Sandler did not seem all that interested anymore. A thought suddenly struck him. "I wonder what Rabbi Sandler would do if I stopped being *frum*? He would come running, I am sure. He would look after us until we became *frum* again." He let his thoughts wander along these lines. The Rabbi's shocked face as he saw him leave a steak-house, as he saw Sandy take off her *sheitel*; and then the undivided attention of both Rabbi and Rebbetsin to make them *frum* again. But this time he would kick back harder, make it more difficult for them. They would have to work a lot harder this time.

He stopped with a jolt as he saw where his thoughts had taken him. He was shocked at himself, and also realized he would be late for work. He had to hurry.

As Michael entered the building, a sudden sense of foreboding overtook him. He tried to brush it off. He wished the secretary a "good morning" and she stared back at him, responding only after some time. What could be wrong with her?

As he walked through the office, people gave him strange, serious looks, said "good morning," and then quickly looked away. What was going on?

Stephen met him at the door of the office. He looked at him steadily and then sighed.

"I don't believe it," he said. "I don't believe it could be true. I have known you for a long time, and I just can't believe it."

"What are you talking about?" Michael asked, feeling a hot flush take over his face and neck.

"That printout we did for you, the Selby printout," Stephen said. "There was something very wrong with it."

Still flushed, Michael explained to Stephen exactly what had happened, how he had been playing with the figures, had been suddenly called away to the hospital, and how the firm had requested a printout of the figures while he was gone. He was glad to get it off his chest.

Stephen looked relieved but worried. "Everyone believes you took the money and then altered the figures."

"But would I have taken it? Where would I have put it?" Michael asked, totally enmeshed in the horror of what was happening.

"Probably in a bank account under another name, or in a Swiss bank account where you can just go by a number."

"But there would be a record of that," Michael protested.

"By typing in those figures, you proved you can eradicate records."

"But I didn't *steal* the money!"

"I know," Stephen said. "But you still eradicated the record of the theft. We can't trace where it went, especially after all this time."

"You believe that I'm guilty," said Michael softly. "You don't believe what I'm telling you."

"Michael, I believe you, I really do. I've known you a long time, and I know that you're an honest man. But Michael, not another soul on earth would believe you."

It suddenly dawned on Michael that everything Stephen said rang true. By typing in those figures he had incriminated himself deeply — very deeply. In fact, the evidence against him was now possibly overwhelming.

He sat down heavily at his desk and put his head in his hands. What could be worse? He was branded as a thief. And he was *frum*. It was a *chilul Hashem*. He felt tears coming into his eyes and brushed them away. Men don't cry, do they? He felt a heavy, black cloud of suspicion pressing down on him.

"I'll tell them about this," Stephen finally said. "I'll tell them what happened. Perhaps we can find some proof. I wish you hadn't typed in those figures, though."

"But I didn't mean to use them at all. I just typed them in to see what was wrong — to see if I could get some idea of where the money was going. I got called out right at that point."

"I know, I know," Stephen said. "But who would believe it?" Who, indeed, but himself?

"Listen," Stephen went on. "You didn't take the money, but someone else did. The firm has initiated a police investigation. The police will come up with something."

"I must leave the firm."

"No, you can't, you mustn't. It would just seem to prove your guilt. And besides, instructions were given to everybody that no one is allowed to talk about this outside of the department. Not one word is to leave these four walls, for the sake of security and also for the sake of our name. If this got out, who would trust us with their account?"

"But to work here, under this cloud?"

"Yes," Stephen said. "Michael, you have to. I will be here for you."

Stephen walked away, leaving Michael feeling totally desolate.

Who could he turn to? Who would understand?

He found himself dialing Rabbi Sandler's number.

Sandy was shocked when Michael confided to her what had happened at the office. How could anyone suspect her husband? But, being an optimist, she consoled herself with the thought that everything would come right in the end. They decided not to tell Grandpa because he would worry.

"Do many people know about this?" she asked Michael.

"I don't think so. They are trying to keep it quiet. I mean, it isn't the kind of thing you will hear at your book club, if that's what you mean."

"You don't know my book club," she thought wryly. Thank goodness she would not be going for the next two weeks.

There was a meeting of the book club the very next day. It was good Sandy wasn't there.

"Are you sure? Did you really hear that? I can't believe it!" Pat's blue eyes were wide with amazement. "Are you absolutely sure?"

"I heard it from someone who usually knows what's going on," Maureen said, looking at Pat carefully. "In fact, I've only told you a fraction of what I heard. The rest, of course, is confidential. I couldn't tell you about that."

"About what?" Diane asked, joining them.

"It's amazing," Pat said. "I can't believe it. Maureen, can I tell her?"

"I would rather you didn't," Maureen said. "I am sure Pamela didn't want me to repeat anything. Her husband would be furious. He told her that he wasn't supposed to tell her because it was just a suspicion, and it would give the firm a bad name. But he wanted to share it with her because he knew he had to tell someone, and of course she promised faithfully she wouldn't repeat it."

"But you told me," said Pat.

"Not much," Maureen retorted. "I didn't tell you the real crux of the matter. Anyway," she added, as she saw that Diane had no intention of leaving, "anyway, I'm going to get myself another cup of tea. Anyone else want something?"

"Another of those cookies, thanks," Diane said. "One of those chocolate ones, those round chocolate ones. I shouldn't really be eating them but..."

"But they are delicious," said Pat. "They really are. I've had three already. Can you get me another one, too?" she called after Maureen.

"Now tell me what she said," Diane said quickly. "She won't know you are telling me."

"Do you think I should?" began Pat. "I mean..."

"She won't be long," Diane said. "If you are going to tell

me you had better tell me quickly. You don't usually keep things from me."

Pat hesitated, doubtful, her lips slightly parted. Suddenly she looked up. "I keep things confidential," she said.

"Of course you do," said Diane. "But it's just a matter of time before everyone knows anyway. Look, there's Maureen coming back... Oh, but she's stopped to talk to Beverley. Come on, who's it about?"

"Oh, I suppose I can tell you just that," said Pat, flicking back her short, fair curls. "It's actually about Sandy."

"Sandy!" exclaimed Diane, in wonderment. "Sandy! I thought she was beyond...I mean, she is so religious!"

"I didn't say anything about her," Pat said, a little irritated.

"Come on, what about her? Maureen will be here in a minute. What has she done wrong?"

"It's not her, it's her husband, Michael. They've found out he's a thief, a big-time thief." Pat blushed as she realized she had probably said too much.

"But he is religious," Diane said. "I am amazed, I truly am. You know more?"

"Of course I do," Pat said. "I know much more, much more. But I can't tell you about it," she said piously.

At that moment Maureen joined them, and, feeling guilty, they both overdid their effusive thanks for the chocolate cookies she had brought. Pat started talking about the new neighbor on the block and how everyone had accepted her, not realizing that her background was not all that it appeared to be. They were soon deep into their discussion, tearing apart one person after another. Sandy, however, was not mentioned. The subject really was taboo.

Diane looked at her watch. "Wow, look at the time. I have to pick up the kids from play school. Don't any of you have to hurry?"

"My kids come home with a car pool," Dorothy said. "I can wait for a while. Anyway, I have to go to the supermarket. I have things to get for the party tonight."

"What party?" Wendy asked. Dorothy was supposed to be a good friend of hers, and she hadn't heard anything about it.

"It's just my husband's business friends."

"I'm going to get the children," announced Diane again, this time deliberately picking up her car keys and walking towards the door.

Pat followed her outside.

"Tell me more about Michael," Diane said as they got to the cars.

"I thought you were in a hurry," said Pat.

"Well, I am, but not such a hurry that I can't listen to everything you have to say. Tell me all about it."

Pat paused, embarrassed. What did she know for sure?

"Don't leave anything out," Diane said.

Pat sprung to her original defense. "Look, it's really confidential," she said. "I'll ask Maureen if I can tell you, and at the same time I'll try to find out more details."

"You can at least tell me what he stole. Did he actually go into someone's house or business?"

"No, nothing like that," said Pat. "It was apparently all done on computer."

"Oh, that's not so bad," Diane said.

"But it was a lot of money."

"But it wasn't as if he held up someone and took it," Diane said. She would have to ask some of her friends to see what they thought of this.

"You will keep this confidential," said Pat.

"Of course. What do you expect?" Diane said. This was really something she had to tell her friends, especially Hilda, who hadn't been there that day. Her husband was into computers. She would be very interested. What a scandal, all happening to the family who wouldn't even eat in other people's houses. That showed something, didn't it!

CHAPTER 9

I think I should leave and go away. I'm no good to anyone." Michael was pale, and he had dark, puffy rings under his eyes. He looked as if he might have been crying.

"Where should we go?" whispered Sandy.

"No, I don't mean you and the kids. I'm the one who has to leave."

"You?" asked Sandy. She noticed tiny wrinkles that had appeared over the last few days around Michael's mouth, tiny lines of bitterness and pain. "How long would you go away for?"

"Forever!" he said, his voice cracking a little. "You would be better off without me. You don't want to be attached to a criminal. The children don't need a father who is a thief."

"But you're not a thief, Michael."

"I'm condemned already," Michael's voice sounded flat and defeated. "Don't worry, I'll find work somewhere and I'll send money to you regularly. You won't starve. It's just that I can't stay here anymore."

"Michael, don't say that. We're a family, and where you

go, we go, too. Wherever we go, we'll be together."

Michael shook his head. "You can't want to stay with me."

"How can you say that? I'm your wife. That isn't even a question. If you decided to leave and go somewhere else, we would all go with you."

"How can you want to be with me after I made such a mess of things?"

"But you haven't made a mess of things at all! It wasn't your fault."

"I shouldn't have typed those numbers in."

"But that's the way you work things out. Even I can see that, and I've never really worked with figures. Michael, we are your family. You can't leave us."

"I don't know what to do," he said.

"Have you spoken to Rabbi Sandler?" she asked.

"A little, but I don't know if he understands. Maybe he thinks I did it, too."

"I think he is a better judge of character than that," said Sandy.

Michael thought for a moment. "I spoke to him on the phone. Perhaps I should go and see him. I know he has been trying to talk to me about it."

"Why have you been avoiding him?" asked his wife, guessing at the answer.

Michael's voice sounded weary. "It's just that we used to be so close, and he was so caring, and getting into *Yiddishkeit* was so exciting and now..."

"The sparkle has gone?" suggested Sandy.

"Yes, I suppose you could say something like that."

"And you feel it has something to do with the Rabbi?"

"Uh, no, that is..." His voice hardened. "Yes, it is his fault. A person makes you *frum* and then...they drop you, just like that. They wait till you become totally committed and change your life and start doing all kinds of things you would never have dreamed of doing before. You become all hyped up and ready to go, and then the Rabbi disappears and starts concentrating on new people to make *frum* and then drop." He said this with an intensity which startled them both, but once he had started he couldn't stop.

"A few years ago I was able to eat anything I wanted anywhere I wanted. I could shop on Saturdays and go to the cinema in the afternoon. I was free. We were all free. But then we became inspired by this *Yiddishkeit* thing. We became dazzled by Rabbi Sandler. And look at us. We are keeping Shabbos, kashrus, everything else. You are wearing a *sheitel*. The kids are in Jewish schools learning stuff I thought only rabbis had to know. They are growing up this way, all because of Rabbi Sandler!"

"Would you change it?" asked Sandy gently.

He sat down, putting his head in his hands. It was several minutes before he answered.

"No. I would never change it. Of course I would never change it. I wouldn't like to live any other way."

"And the Rabbi?" she asked. "There are other rabbis."

"I wouldn't change the Rabbi either," he said doggedly.

"Then speak to him."

"Yes, yes, I said I was going to. I really will."

"No," she said. "I don't mean only about the missing money. I mean about what you just said to me, about *Yid-*

dishkeit, and about him making people *frum* and then dropping them."

Michael gave a bitter laugh. "Are you crazy?" he asked. "How could I possibly say that to him?"

"You have been showing it to him anyway. By your every action, even in the hospital."

He was again silent for several minutes. "All right, I'll phone him," he said.

The Rabbi led Michael into the office and sat down opposite him. "Please tell me more about what is happening, about the accusations," he began.

Michael flinched. He had, for a few moments, forgotten all about his troubles at work. He needed to get something else off his chest first, something that had bothered him for months and months. He wondered if the Rabbi would ever speak to him again.

Michael twisted uncomfortably in the chair. This was going to be difficult, very difficult. And, also, how would Rabbi Sandler react? Would he be insulted? Would he tell him to go and find himself another rabbi? Even though Michael was deeply upset with him, he couldn't afford to lose him as a rabbi and as a friend.

Rabbi Sandler knew how sensitive Michael was, and he understood how deeply hurt and confused he was about being the object of suspicion. Superficial reassurance would not help. Michael was just not that kind of person. He was in a horrible position, a position which no one would envy.

"These things have a way of working themselves out," Rabbi Sandler finally said. "There must be a real thief somewhere, and we'll just have to wait until he is found. It will be difficult to work with people who suspect you, but you must carry on. You know you are innocent."

Rabbi Sandler read the pain and hurt in Michael's eyes. Michael had not been close to him for the past few months. He seemed to have been avoiding him.

"Michael, could we have a *shiur* together? Could we learn something together? Even if it's twenty minutes a day — perhaps before or after the morning davening. You haven't been coming for a long time now. You aren't as close as before."

It was now or never. Michael's words came out slowly, as if they were being dragged from depths of confusion and despair.

"It isn't me who hasn't been close," he said finally. "It's you. You make people *frum* and then you...you..."

The Rabbi blushed crimson, not with anger, but with something else that Michael couldn't define. He could not finish his sentence, but the Rabbi did it for him. "I make them *frum* and then I drop them."

It was Michael's turn to blush. "Yes," he said at last.

"Why do you think I dropped you?" the Rabbi asked softly.

"I don't know why you dropped me," said Michael. His voice became bitter. "Maybe because we are all *frum* now and there is nothing more to do, and now you can turn your attention to new people and make them *frum*."

He glanced at the Rabbi, aware that he had actually hurt him. He had not meant to do that. He hadn't even thought he was capable of doing that. He had never really thought that rabbis could get hurt, especially not Rabbi Sandler. And if he really thought about it, the Sandlers had been incredibly good to them. Even very recently, with Chanie's illness, they had been there as always.

He began to feel guilty. "I'm sorry," he said. "I really am sorry."

"Michael, you have no idea how glad I am that you told me this. I knew that something was very wrong, but nothing I did would remedy it, and you wouldn't speak to me about it. You put up a barrier that I somehow couldn't break through. You know, you dropped me, too." He smiled.

"I'm sorry," said Michael again.

"Michael, I wish I had known sooner. But then, it's never too late. It's important, very important, for us to discuss this, and we can do so now in an honest way."

Michael, feeling incredibly vulnerable, just nodded.

"When a person first becomes *frum*," said the Rabbi, "everything is exciting, glowing, and challenging. A Jew is discovering his Creator and responding with the deepest elements of his soul. He is taking upon himself more and more mitzvos and binding himself more and more to Hashem. His learning is like water falling on parched earth.

"There is often tremendous opposition from family, friends, and business associates, and that makes the *ba'al teshuvah* cling more to the person who made him *frum*, to the people who encouraged him in his first steps. That is natural. At the same time, the Rabbi has the holy and great responsibility of guiding the person into *Yiddishkeit*."

"Does the responsibility end there?" Michael asked, bitter in spite of himself.

"Absolutely not, Heaven forbid," said Rabbi Sandler. "It actually never ends. But it is different," he added, as Michael was about to protest.

"Let's look at your Chanie and at your other children," he continued. "Chanie needs, and has needed over the last eleven months or so, a great deal of constant attention?"

"That's right," Michael said, almost guessing what the Rabbi was going to say next.

"And your other children. They also need a great deal of attention, but they are older now and they need it in a different way. Attention such as Chanie gets would be detrimental to their emotional and physical development."

Michael nodded.

"And as they get older," the Rabbi continued, "they have to become more independent and we have to stand aside just a little, but at the same time to be very much there."

Michael gave the Rabbi a long look. What he said obviously made a great deal of sense. "I suppose so," he said. A wave of depression threatened to engulf him.

"Michael," continued the Rabbi, "a person has to grow. A person has to have an *emunah* and *bitachon* which is his own. A person has to learn and daven and deepen to a point where he is permeated more and more with *Yiddishkeit*.

"You could help me a lot, Michael, in all sorts of ways. You can give a great deal. You have come from a non-*frum* background, and to some people what you can say about *Yiddishkeit* is more powerful than a rabbi's words."

"Maybe," Michael said, "but not anymore. Now I'm nothing but a thief."

"We must talk more, at length," said the Rabbi, "and regularly. In the meanwhile, is that *shiur* on? Will you come?"

"I'll come," said Michael. "And we can learn together."

And so it was arranged.

Michael was rather confused, however, by Rabbi Sandler's parting words:

"And thank you, Michael, for referring Richard to me. I feel we will get somewhere. He is basically a good kid, and he's been through a lot."

He wondered what had happened. Probably Sandy had told him about the Rabbi. But when, and why?

His own problems were too pressing for him to think long about it, however, and it was only later on in the evening that he suddenly remembered the Rabbi's comment and questioned Sandy.

No, she had not told Richard to go to the Rabbi. She had never even spoken to Richard at length. Perhaps Daniel had done so. But Daniel was asleep now. She would ask him about it the next day.

But by then, it had slipped her mind.

As the days passed, Michael found it more and more difficult to work. The atmosphere in the office became colder and colder. Only Stephen remained a firm friend. Without him, he would not have been able to stay there.

He was learning with the Rabbi and attending the morning minyan, and he was finding that this was the only truly meaningful part of the day. Strangely enough, when life around him was becoming intolerable, regular Torah study was opening up within him a dimension which he hadn't really known existed.

The Rabbi gave Michael a short program of learning to continue on his own and this, too, was becoming meaningful. In the past he felt he hadn't had time to concentrate on learning. Now it became something to cling to.

At the same time, Michael had become extremely quiet at home. Grandpa kept asking if anything was wrong and if he could do anything about it, but they preferred not to worry him.

It never occurred to them to say anything to the children.

One afternoon, however, Daniel came home with a bleeding nose, scratches, and his clothes torn. He had obviously been in a fight at school. He refused to tell anyone what had caused it.

Later on in the day, however, Sandy found him lying miserably in his bed, staring at the ceiling.

"What's wrong?" Sandy asked. "Tell me what happened. I won't be angry."

"You won't be angry, you'll be upset."

Sandy sat patiently by the bed. She knew that Daniel would eventually confide in her, but, as with Michael, it took time.

"Mommy, they said that Daddy is a thief. A whole lot of them said that, so I attacked them."

Sandy felt her heart sinking. So everybody did know. What could she say to the child? What would sound convincing? Probably only the truth, and she explained to him in brief what had happened.

Daniel looked relieved. Obviously he had heard part of the story from his classmates, and what she told him clarified his father's side of it.

"It will sort itself out," he said. "I know it will. Dad would never, ever do a thing like that." With that, the subject was dropped.

But how long could the family live like this? Something had to happen to prove Michael's innocence.

Grandpa could not be distracted for long, and soon he, too, was demanding an explanation of what was going on.

"The atmosphere has changed around here," he said. "There is something wrong, and I want to know what it is."

"Grandpa, I wanted to talk to you about it," Sandy said, "but I just don't know how."

Grandpa looked at Sandy steadily for a few seconds and then closed the kitchen door. "Tell me, poppet, tell me. I'm glad you're going to tell me at last. I've been hearing hints of what is happening. I know your Michael is in trouble, and I also know he is innocent. He is incapable of doing anything dishonest."

"Grandpa, it's all so terrible. Mike is always so careful with other people's money. He would never have defrauded anyone."

"I know that, my angel, I know," said her grandfather, a slight tremor in his voice. "Did they think he deliberately 'crooked the books'?"

"Grandpa, it was all done on computers," Sandy said. She did not elaborate. How could she? Except for a bit of word processing, she didn't know much about computers at all. And Grandpa definitely didn't. He was from another age completely.

"That's interesting," Grandpa said, "Was the system

connected to the Net?"

"I don't know anything about it," Sandy said, surprised that Grandpa had even asked the question. "You mean the Internet? I doubt it."

"But he must have been linked up to a closed network."

"Grandpa, do you know anything about computers?"

"Oh yes," he said. "In the past few years I've done many things on computers. I started by getting myself an old 286, and then I outgrew that and got hold of a 386DX and that satisfied me for a while. Now, in my apartment, I have a Pentium."

"Windows 95 and all that?" she asked.

"That's right," said Grandpa. "I think I've become something of an addict. I spend many hours every evening on the World Wide Web, and you really can spend many hours on it. More and more it's becoming known as the World Wide Wait. But newsgroups are okay. I have even posted a few comments into them and had several replies to my e-mail address, replies from all over the world."

"Grandpa, I had no idea you knew how to do any of this. They didn't even have computers in your day."

"When was my day?" asked Grandpa, his eyes twinkling. "They have computers now."

He grew serious again. So it was all done on computers. That made it interesting, very, very interesting.

He paused, wishing somehow to comfort his granddaughter. He nodded sympathetically. "But this thing that has happened to Michael...it happened to me a couple of times. Really awful. You don't know what to say, and you know you are innocent.

"One of the times, they found they had made a mistake and they all came and apologized. The other time, I just had to live through it, and eventually I left. All those people are not around anymore, but it still hurts."

Sandy suddenly felt a great relief that such a thing had happened to Grandpa. Twice!

She was glad that she had told him.

"Hey, what's in that box Grandpa's carrying under his arm?" Dina asked as Grandpa walked in with his purchase, a look of satisfaction on his face.

"Now I'm connected," he said, "or I will be very shortly."

Sam almost bounced out of his room. "Grandpa, did you get it? What kind did you get? Can we play games on it?"

"So far only Minesweepers, Solitaire, and Tetris, and maybe a couple of others, but I haven't looked at those yet."

Sandy was staring at him. "You bought...you bought...a computer? Why did you buy a computer?"

"Only a little laptop," Grandpa said. "And a small laser printer. It will go with my cellular phone. I have just joined the most reputable network server, and, presto, I am linked to the outside world."

"And he's got games," said Sam, "and he's letting us play on it."

"Grandpa, it isn't a children's toy," Sandy said. "You can't let them use it."

"Why not? It will improve their education. They need to know how to handle these things."

"Let them do it at school," said Sandy.

"There isn't any teacher as good as personal experience," Grandpa said. "They must learn this on their own."

Lovingly, he unpacked it, surrounded by his granddaughter and her three older children. "Magnificent!" he exclaimed as he took it out of its polystyrenc protection. "Am I glad to have an excuse to buy this. I was really missing my computer."

"Why didn't you say so, Grandpa?" Sandy asked. "I am sure we could have borrowed some kind of computer for you. I didn't know you loved computers so much. I didn't even know you knew how to use one."

The old man was hugging the machine and...talking to it. "You and I are going to solve this mystery," he said, "just you and I, you and I together."

"How are you going to do that?" Sandy asked.

"We are now in contact with the whole world," said Grandpa, still hugging the laptop.

"Hey, Grandpa, you need a mouse," Dina said, coming closer to look.

"We have a built-in mouse," Grandpa said. "See this little touchpad over here? That's our mouse."

"Hey," Daniel said. "You just need to move your finger across it. That's really great."

With a magnificent chord, the computer sprang into action. "Let's see what we have here," Grandpa said excitedly. "I was afraid we wouldn't have battery power, but we do, and we can operate."

For the next three hours, the laptop, and Grandpa, were the undisputed center of attention in the Berman home.

The man stiffened as he read the message. This was im-

possible. He had been convinced that there could be no reper-
cussions. But he had communicated with them, hadn't he?
He had freely given them his e-mail address. Perhaps he
should have listened to Martin. Martin must not know about
this. In no way was Martin ever to know about this.

He shuddered. This thing could get out of hand. It could
follow him, hound him. He was beginning to feel the cold
grip of terror.

He read the message again. It was from Jip, the man who
had posted him the original software to access the Selby
account.

> Good evening sir. I congratulate you on
> your success. I have spent some time
> sniffing around your hard disk and I am
> finding it fascinating, especially the
> letters to your bank just before we made
> contact. I am sure they respect you now
> as a wealthy member of society. You do
> realize that what I gave you is share-
> ware; not in the usual sense, but in the
> sense that we have now become partners,
> and in this respect we share the prof-
> its. We really must come to some ar-
> rangement. I spotted your talent and
> your interest the moment you posted to
> the newsgroup. Congratulations to a wor-
> thy member of the team.

He didn't want to look at this. It made him uncomfortable, very uncomfortable. Which team was he supposed to be
a member of? He didn't like it one bit.

CHAPTER 10

Michael stiffened. It was becoming a nightmare. How could this be happening to him, of all people? Why did he have to go through this? Why should *anyone* have to go through this?

He had heard the voices inside the main office. He hadn't imagined it. He hadn't imagined it at all. These men were policemen. He could hear snatches of what they were saying. Had they come to arrest him? Was he on his way to jail? His heart started to beat faster and faster, and he felt sure that anyone who stood close to him would hear it. That would make him appear more guilty, wouldn't it? A guilty man always reacted to the police. But then, so did an innocent man, surely.

His hands were clammy and hot, and he had to hold them to stop them from trembling. He knew he was doomed. The three men came into his office, closing the door behind them. He hadn't been imagining it. Although dressed in regular clothes, they *looked* like policemen, spoke like policemen.

"Sergeant Roberts and Sergeant Masanga," announced the tallest of the three. "I am Captain Engelbrecht from the

South African Crime Investigation Unit."

Michael motioned them to sit in the other three chairs in his office and sat down a little away from his desk. How could one be interrogated by policemen while sitting behind one's desk? His mouth had become completely dry so that he doubted he could speak. He desperately wished he had some water to drink.

"You are Mr. Michael Berman?" the captain began.

"Yes, yes, I am," Michael said, feeling sure that his voice was thick from the dryness of his mouth.

"Would you prefer to have your lawyer present?" asked the captain. Obviously it was necessary for him to say this.

"I...I don't have a lawyer," said Michael. "I have never been to a lawyer...in my life."

"I would advise you very strongly, Mr. Berman, to get yourself a lawyer. In fact I would advise you to get yourself the best lawyer you can find. This is a very serious matter involving a great deal of money. The penalties are extremely severe."

Michael's head felt as if it was about to burst. He hadn't even considered getting a lawyer. "I hoped your investigations would make it unnecessary for me to do that," said Michael.

The policeman was watching him carefully. "We are uncovering more and more evidence against you," he said slowly.

Michael felt ill. He blushed crimson.

"It isn't only the Selby account," the policeman went on. "There are other accounts, some that you are not dealing with directly. There are also gold cards and other credit cards which are being used fraudulently. We are finding that these

things are tying up. It is the same mastermind behind everything. *You*," he said ominously.

"I have only dealt with the Selby account," Michael answered quietly.

"You admit that?" said the policeman sharply.

"Yes, I do. That is common knowledge. Everyone knows
that I was working with that account."

"And you falsified the figures," said the captain. "We
have proof of that, absolute proof of that."

"I didn't falsify them," said Michael. "I just..."

"You typed in figures that were incorrect," said the man.

"Yes I did, I did, I know I did."

"Then you admit your guilt?" The policeman sounded
surprised.

"No, I am not guilty. I didn't take any money."

"But your accomplice did, and you shared it," the policeman accused.

Michael tried to explain. "I saw that there were large
amounts of money missing from the Selby account. I wanted
to work backwards to see how it could have occurred, so I
typed in some figures to make the amounts look regular
again and tried to work backwards and see what the problem
was. I am sure that many accountants would do the same."

"And what did you find when you worked backwards?"
the policeman asked quietly.

"I never got to finish. I just typed in the figures and then
when I was about to work with them I got a message from the
hospital that my baby was ill, that her life was in danger. So I
logged off and left immediately for the hospital."

"Very convenient, Mr. Berman. Do you honestly believe

anyone would buy that?"

"That is what happened," Michael said. "I promise you, it's the truth."

"They all promise," the policeman said, glancing at his colleagues, Sergeant Masanga wearing an expression of interest and Sergeant Roberts exhibiting something akin to contempt.

"How long did you stay at the hospital?" the captain asked.

"A couple of hours," Michael said, "maybe even three or four."

"Then you went back to work?"

"Yes I did, " said Michael, knowing he was not going to be able to explain his subsequent actions.

"Then what happened when you worked back from those figures?"

"I...I didn't. I didn't get a chance to do that. Someone had already printed out the figures for the Selby account."

"The figures that you typed in?"

"Yes, that's right. The figures...they had printed them out together with the figures I had typed in."

"So everything looked perfect with Selby," said the policeman.

"Yes, it did," Michael said.

"There was no record of the missing money?"

"Not on that printout."

"So you had covered your tracks, hadn't you, Mr. Berman? You had covered your tracks very well. You never even reported it. You realize I could have you arrested immediately."

The captain put his face close to Michael's. "Tell us who you were working with, Mr. Berman. You know, if you turn State Witness and testify against your colleagues, the sentence could be a little lighter. I see you are not a person who is used to crime. We know our hardened criminals."

"Then if I am not that type, why don't you believe me?" Michael asked.

"Mr. Berman," the captain answered, mustering a friendly tone, "you do see that your story sounds ridiculous. Here you type in figures, which makes the crime impossible to detect, then you are suddenly called away to the hospital just before you can 'work backwards,' as you say. And then someone prints out your work without your consent and sends it on to the firm. You apparently come back from the hospital, find that the account has been printed out, and you say nothing, absolutely nothing. You allow the figures to go through, to be accepted."

Michael blushed. True, he had done exactly that. Why had he done that? Of that he definitely was guilty. But was that a crime? It probably was. He had committed a crime in covering up a crime. But he hadn't committed that original crime, and he hadn't worked as anyone's accomplice. Of that he was innocent.

"You realize there is no way out," the policeman said. "Tell us who you were working with."

"Nobody," said Michael.

"So you pulled this off all by yourself."

"No, no, I didn't! I didn't pull anything off. I just typed in the figures."

"That is fraud," the policeman declared.

"A lot of accountants do it," Michael said. "It is one way of working out a problem."

"A fraudulent way of working out a problem," the captain stated grimly. He had obviously made up his mind. "In the old South Africa we would have had ways to loosen up your tongue. Under the new regime we can't use those methods anymore. But we will find a way, we surely will. We have other methods now." His light blue eyes glinted.

"I am not guilty of any crime," Michael repeated.

"Oh, but you are! By your own admission you are. At the very least you suppressed evidence of a crime. It is against the law to suppress evidence." His words were threatening.

Sergeant Masanga spoke. "Mr. Berman, do you have any idea who could have committed this crime?" His voice held a note of genuine concern, and Michael immediately responded to it.

"Sergeant, I don't know. I thought I could find out myself. I wanted to work on it. I just needed a few days to think about it."

"You hoped it would all go away, get brushed under the carpet — the money gone and the shareholders depleted," said the captain.

"Yes I did, in a way, or rather, I knew it had to be found out but I hoped it would be in some other way, not through our offices."

"It *was* discovered in some other way. But of course your figures were there with an attempt to cover up the situation."

Sergeant Roberts had been writing for several minutes. He handed the statement to the captain, who read it slowly. Eventually he handed it to Michael.

"You will sign this," he said. "It is simply a statement of what you have told us."

"Perhaps I *should* get a lawyer," Michael said.

"As you please," the captain said, looking a little bored.

Michael read the statement through. It seemed to be a fair assessment of what he had said to them, and without thinking further he signed it. He wasn't a criminal. Surely that would be obvious to anyone. He could not damage himself by signing a statement.

For some reason, Captain Engelbrecht looked triumphant. "Thank you, Mr. Berman. You will be hearing from us shortly. You will agree that you signed this statement willingly and without pressure. If you please, sign that for us."

Michael immediately became suspicious. Perhaps he *did* need a lawyer. Could he really trust the police? Were they trying to incriminate him?

He tried to pull himself together. The police were surely to be trusted. They would find the real criminal. They *had* to. They wouldn't leave him trapped by his own admission. Had he committed a crime? Somehow he knew he hadn't.

But he had signed the statement, and they hadn't used force.

Captain Engelbrecht was holding a piece of paper in front of him. He signed it, barely reading it. Yes, he would have to see a lawyer right away. He didn't even know any lawyers.

He would have to find one in the telephone directory.

It was some weeks later that Jerry Cohen, Richard's father, knocked at the door. Jerry might have been good looking if he hadn't had a drinker's bloated face. One might have noticed the large grey eyes framed by long eyelashes, the square chin which should have stood for strength, and the rather pronounced mouth.

Michael was surprised to see him. He had been fairly friendly with the Cohens when they first moved in, but both families had realized that they had very little in common and had drifted apart, with just a curt "good morning" being exchanged between them.

Only Richard had remained friendly with Daniel. But he had not been over for weeks, maybe even months. Michael had seen him at *shul*, though, in the mornings, putting on *tefillin*. Strange, he had never thought he had any interest in being religious. He seemed to be somewhat different now.

"I wanted to come and chat with you," Jerry said. "Do you have a few minutes?"

"Certainly," Michael answered, welcoming him into the lounge. Sandy went to make them some coffee.

"I know this must seem strange to you," Jerry began. "Especially as we haven't had much contact lately. But I have been watching you and your family for a very long time.

"At first your religion made me angry," he continued, "and I didn't want to see it happening next door to me. I would watch you burning *chametz* just before Pesach and that would annoy me more than anything, I'm not sure why. And your *sukkah*, and your singing. But then it started to get to me, and I would still be annoyed but at the same time I wished that our family could be like yours.

"Ours is hardly a family any longer. We don't know one another. None of us seems to have anything to say anymore.

There is no time like your Shabbos, that we are all together.

"But there has recently been a change in my son, Richard. Since that Rabbi took him under his wing, he has become more of a mensch. He talks to me, he even really seems to be fond of me. He is changing, and he is becoming more and more religious — slowly, but very definitely — and he is becoming very much nicer with it.

"I have been watching your family, and on many occasions I have found them an inspiration. And you yourself, Michael, you seem to be so at peace."

Michael winced at this. How much further could this be from the truth?

"I would like to learn from you, Michael," he was saying. "Maybe it's not too late."

Michael was stunned. He was having his own crisis in *Yiddishkeit* and in his life in general, and here was someone asking for his help.

"Jerry, why don't you go talk to Rabbi Sandler?"

"I will go to the Rabbi," Jerry said. "But there are things I would rather learn from someone who has been through it all. After all, a Rabbi has to be religious, it's his job. But you don't have to, and you are."

Why am I hesitating? thought Michael. A year ago I would have jumped at the chance of making someone *frum*. He said, however, "Of course I will help you in any way I can."

But what could he offer?

Sandy had heard the last part of the conversation. "What about your whole family eating with us on a Friday night?"

Jerry gave a smile. "I can only answer for Richard and myself. We will definitely come, and I will start going to *shul* with Richard sometimes. We need a change."

They chatted for some time, Jerry telling him about his work, his office, his holiday, and so on.

"He's a nice guy, " Michael said after he had gone. "If he would stop drinking so much, he could be a good friend."

Sandy agreed. She was glad Michael had something else to think about. He had come home from work devastated. The police had been questioning him again, and again he had to repeat the story of what had happened. He had been to a lawyer that afternoon — he had made an appointment with him shortly after that first police visit. The meeting was a bitter disappointment. He thought again of the painful experience:

"Mr. Berman, it would have been far better for all of us if you hadn't signed anything at all. I just wish you had come to me in the first place. One has to know how to deal with these things."

Michael sighed. How was he supposed to know how to behave when accused of a crime?

"The fact that you admitted to typing in those numbers," said the lawyer, "that was not a good idea, not a good idea at all. That incriminates you fairly heavily."

"But I *did* type in those numbers," Michael said.

"Mr. Berman, it is important for people to believe you are innocent!"

Suddenly Michael realized that the lawyer, even the lawyer, didn't believe him. "I will have to get another lawyer," he said quickly. "You don't believe me, and you can't defend me."

The young man looked a little taken aback. He wasn't used to such statements from clients. All the evidence was against Mr. Berman. Surely he could not be innocent. "I will defend you even if you are guilty of a crime," he said a little stiffly.

"I don't want that," said Michael. "I would rather be without a lawyer."

"This consultation will cost you, Mr. Berman. You can spend a few days thinking about what you have just said."

Michael hesitated. How many more lawyers was he going to see? How much more money was he going to have to spend? He looked around the luxurious office of Leonard Wilkinson and Partners. The man opposite him was obviously one of the partners, one of the junior partners — a smug, self-satisfied young man in a two thousand rand suit.

Michael hesitated. Why was he getting so angry with him? He had no reason and no right to do that. "I'm sorry," Michael said. "I will have to think about it. I really must think about it."

"I will leave the case open," said the man who called himself Peter Durrant. "When you are ready to come clean, we can talk."

Michael emerged from the rooms feeling tattered and overcome with a sense of horror and disgust. The lawyer didn't believe him. He was asking him to admit guilt to something he would never dream of doing.

He went back to the office only to face again the antagonistic stares of the staff. Why did everyone think he was a criminal? Did he act like one?

He entered his office and closed the door. A place which had often been so pleasant for him to be in now held only suspicion and fear. The very walls were beginning to exude cold terror.

Why didn't they believe him? Because he was the most likely suspect. He had tampered with the figures.

The other staff members stared at him as he walked through the offices after the police visit. He had been friendly with them. He had helped some of them with their work. He had talked with them, joked with them. He had never been irritable or angry or rude to any of them. And now — they were facing him with a stony silence. He knew they were talking a great deal about him behind his back, but no one spoke to him directly.

Only Stephen was warm and friendly, and Michael began to realize that Stephen, too, was being punished for his friendship with Michael. He, too, often encountered a stony silence from the rest of the staff.

Michael had wanted to leave more than once, but Stephen insisted he wait it out until his name was cleared.

"Then we will both leave," he had said, much to Michael's surprise.

"Why are you putting yourself on the line for me?" Michael had asked.

"Michael, you have always been a good friend, and that doesn't change. But the answer really goes back to what happened when I was about twelve years old, when I had just started in a new school.

"I wasn't a healthy child. I became ill with pneumonia

and had all kinds of complications with it. I missed a lot of school, and there were many things I wasn't allowed to do.

"The other boys in the school used to tease me, and some even started to punch me. I didn't want to tell my family, and, though I have now learned karate, there was no way that I could defend myself then.

"There was a Jewish boy in the school. His name was Raymond. He wasn't much older than I was, and one day he saw one of the older boys picking on me. He took the boy aside and I don't know what happened after that, but the punching stopped. He must have spoken to the boys in my class also, because they stopped teasing me, and whenever I had a problem, he always seemed to be around. I will never forget him."

Stephen had a faraway look in his eyes. Michael found it hard to believe that Stephen had ever been a "weakling." He now went jogging every morning and kept himself very fit.

Michael felt somehow grateful to that unknown Raymond who had protected Stephen so many years before.

CHAPTER 11

Grandpa was glad to hear that at least part of the Cohen family would be with them on Shabbos evening. "If Richard is coming," he said to Michael and Sandy, "that means that he has managed to get off drugs. He made me a promise. And he has been going to the Rabbi, as I told him to."

"You told him, Grandpa?" Sandy asked, surprised. "You aren't even religious!"

"It might come as a surprise to you," he said, a distant look coming into his eyes, "but everything you are doing here was once second-nature to me. For weeks now, it's been tugging at my memory, bringing things up from the past. Things that were part of my life a long, long time ago.

"As you know, back in the old country, I was the eldest of eight children. We learned, we davened, we wore *tzitzis*, we put on *tefillin*. We studied *Chumash* with *Rashi*. We had a Rav, we asked him *sheilos*. My father, may his memory be blessed, was a shop owner, but he would spend hours learning Gemara, and my mother, of blessed memory, always kept her hair covered. She baked challah, she lit Shabbos candles.

"Shabbos in the old country was magnificent. My father at the head of the table, my mother like a queen, all of us feeling like princes and princesses. We struggled, yes. We didn't have much money, or anything 'fancy' to eat. But on Shabbos, everything tasted different.

"I never again experienced a Shabbos like that, until I came here. And then I see my great grandchildren doing the things I used to do, things which I thought were dead, out-of-date, and of no consequence."

Grandpa paused and took a long drink from his coffee cup.

"When I came to this country many, many years ago, I came by myself, and I felt as if I had the whole world in front of me. The boat ride over had been difficult but exciting. We were still religious on the ship. There was a minyan, there was davening. In fact, I hadn't even imagined life could be different, until some people on the boat said that the new country was different and that Hashem and *Yiddishkeit* had to be left behind on the boat.

"I couldn't believe this because I had never been exposed to any other kind of life, but when I left the boat and made contact with some of my old friends who had emigrated earlier, I found that they had changed. Oh, how they had changed! They were no longer covering their heads. They kept only part of Shabbos. Girls who had been very, very religious and had married, had taken off their *sheitels* and their scarves and were wearing dresses which we would have been shocked by back in the old country.

"I tried to tell myself that I would be different, and in fact for nearly a year I joined with some yeshivah students who were trying to swim against the tide. But I wasn't a yeshivah student.

"I went to work for a tailor and he kept pressing me to work on Shabbos, and everyone called me a 'greena' and slowly, very slowly and reluctantly, I began to drop this and drop that.

"It was as if you were in the army and you were the only person who seemed to be out of step. Or as if everyone was wearing blue and you were wearing yellow — you sort of stood out — and everyone laughed at you. Not in a spiteful way, in a sort of good-natured way, as if you would 'grow up sometime' and learn to be modern.

"You don't know the pressure, walking around, being laughed at, being made a fool of, and then the camaraderie as I let things go.

"I will never forget the first time I broke Shabbos: The shop was extremely busy, and I was working on a suit for a very important customer. It had to be ready for a business luncheon on Shabbos, midday. I was not quite finished. Now, someone could have finished it for me, but this was the opportunity that maybe, unconsciously, I had been searching for.

"I worked till nine o'clock that night. Shabbos had started at six. I just carried on working...and nothing happened. There were no explosions, the earth didn't rend apart, I didn't get struck by a bolt of lightning. But in another way, something earth-shattering had happened to me and to my *neshamah* — though I didn't realize it. I suppose the 'modem' was becoming faulty but I wasn't aware there was anything wrong with it."

"What did you say, Grandpa?"

"The *neshamah*, you know what a *neshamah* is, surely. It is a soul, a Jewish soul!"

"I know that," Sandy said quickly. "But you said something about a modem, and that was way before they had computers."

"It surely was," he said, laughing. "It most certainly, surely was. It was just the best example I could give to describe the situation. The modem connects the computer to the telephone and then to the whole world. If something is wrong with the modem you just don't connect properly. When I broke Shabbos, although I carried on for a while davening and putting on *tefillin* and everything, I had essentially damaged the modem and the connection was different."

"Though it is never completely broken," Sandy whispered.

Grandpa smiled, and continued.

"People gave me approving looks so it didn't feel so bad, and from then on I broke Shabbos whenever it was inconvenient to keep it; and then I stopped being careful with kashrus and so on and so on.

"I made some fortunes, and lost a few. All in all, I was very successful. I could bring up my family in the lap of luxury — giving them everything I never had. But I never was able to give them what I *did* have: the heritage that my parents would have died for. And I realize, now, that perhaps it really was worth dying for, and living for...."

CHAPTER 12

There was a knock at the door late Thursday evening. Jerry stood there. He had been drinking but wasn't drunk, and he looked upset.

"May I come in?" he asked Sandy, who had opened the door. "I am sorry, I've had a few drinks, but I didn't know what else to do." He started to shake and covered his face with his hands.

Michael led him to a chair. There was silence for a few minutes.

"She's leaving me," Jerry said. "She's leaving and going away."

Michael was silent. He had been expecting this for many months.

"What happened?" he asked.

"Last night I came home late. I had been drinking quite a bit, and I got into a conversation at the bar, and time just went on and on, and I came home very late, and we had words. I don't even remember what words. But something just snapped and I broke a few things. And then I went to bed.

"I woke up late and no one was home, so I got dressed and went to work. I managed okay with my work. A bit of a headache and my stomach felt queasy, but I managed okay. Then I came home, but instead of supper, there was just a note on the table saying I wouldn't be seeing her again, except once more — in court — as soon as possible. And of course I went to the bar and had a few drinks, but something stopped me from drinking a lot, and instead of making me feel better, the drinking just made me feel worse and worse. So I went home again, but the house was still empty — and now I have come to you."

Michael tried to be straightforward, but tactful.

"Do you think your drinking was the problem?" he asked.

"Not at all," said Jerry. "What's wrong with having a few drinks with the boys?" He looked genuinely puzzled, as if he couldn't understand how Michael could have suggested such a thing.

Sandy had come into the room.

"Did Elise ever say anything about your drinking upsetting her?" she asked.

"Oh yes, constantly. She went on and on about it. Said she couldn't take it. But I can control how much I drink. I never get drunk, at least, not really drunk."

Sandy went into the kitchen and Michael cleared his throat, preparing to speak.

"I think you have a problem, " he said.

"Now," said Jerry, suddenly indignant, "don't speak bad of me. I never speak bad of you. In the bar when the guys tell me, 'your neighbor — you think he is a saint — well, all he is is a thief,' I defend you, I do. I tell them I don't believe a word of it."

Michael had turned as white as a sheet, and it took him some seconds before he could speak again.

"Thanks, Jerry," he said.

At that moment, Sandy came back with a plate of steaming hot food.

"Here Jerry, I presume you haven't eaten properly all day. This should make you feel better at least."

Jerry forgot everything else and ate hungrily.

"I forgot to eat," he said. "But who will make breakfast? And sandwiches? And supper?"

"Well," Sandy said, "tomorrow is Friday and you are eating with us. Who else in your family is coming?"

Jerry frowned. "Well, Elise is not here, and of course Tanya is with her. Richard must be here. His school case was at home when I got back."

"Shouldn't you go and see where Richard is?" Sandy asked.

"No," Jerry said. "He knows how to take care of himself. He has a key, so he will be in tonight, sometime. We never worry about him. He will find something to eat, somewhere."

Sandy checked herself from saying anything. Richard was still a child in many ways, and yet his father did not seem to have any interest at all in what he was doing. Small wonder that he had begun to take drugs.

"Have you any idea where Elise would be?" asked Michael.

"Oh, probably at her mother's place. Women usually go to their mothers in these circumstances, don't they?

She must be there," Jerry said, feeling far more confident after a good meal.

"Has she left you before?" Sandy asked.

"She has threatened many times," Jerry said. "But this is the first time she has actually done it. I hope she doesn't stay away too long. I don't know how we will get food."

He got up and walked somewhat unsteadily to the door. "See you tomorrow night, then, with Richard."

> I'm getting impatient. You owe me. Did you think you were in this all by yourself? I have been sniffing your hard drive. You have been making all kinds of financial transactions. You've been moving around hundreds of thousands of rands and dollars. Half of that belongs to me.

The man read this with irritation. Why did this Jip keep hounding him? He had already organized money for him, a great deal of money. Now he wanted more?

He would stall him, put him off. Now, which e-mail address had he used this time? How many more e-mail addresses did Jip possess, or did he perhaps enter and use other people's e-mails? He had heard of it being done before.

Who was Jip? He was a blackmailer and a pest, that he knew. How had he attached himself to him? Jip was surely not his real name. Surely he could find him somehow!

He logged off, thoroughly shaken but with a grim sense of determination. Whoever Jip was, wherever he was — he had to escape him somehow.

CHAPTER 13

Sandy lit the Shabbos candles and looked for a few seconds at the flames. She had always been fascinated by the candles, by the flames which seemed to reflect an eternity. This was a special moment.

She had lit Shabbos candles even before they became *frum*, ever since they had married, but she had often lit them after dark and blown them out after an hour or so. It had been like a "tribute to Shabbos" rather than a welcoming in of a real Shabbos, but even at that stage it had been an important part of her weekly routine.

She went to put the final touches on the Shabbos table, looking with some apprehension at the extra places she had set. She was not sure which guest she was more uneasy about, Richard or his father. Both had massive problems, and she was not sure she could deal with them.

She hoped that they realized what Shabbos was, that it was different and special and that it was not just an invitation to supper. But then it struck her that if they knew little or nothing about Shabbos, it was up to Michael and herself to somehow convey to them some of its beauty.

She remembered how she had felt spending their first Shabbos with the Rabbi. Everything had been touched by an atmosphere of inspiration which conveyed the spirit of Shabbos in a way that nothing else could. Was her family able to convey to someone else the spirit of Shabbos? The possibility seemed to overawe her. Perhaps it was something only a rabbi and his family could do.

Michael had gone to *shul* with the boys, and she was left with baby Chanie, Dina, and Grandpa. Grandpa was resting. He seemed to be needing a lot of rest these days. This was hardly surprising, seeing that he worked long into the night on his computer. What was he doing?

She hoped that Michael and the boys would be home before Jerry and Richard arrived. She felt restless and a little nervous. She tried to settle down to read a book.

She supposed she should be reading a Jewish book, seeing it was Shabbos, but she did want to see what was happening in the novel she had been reading for the past few days. Would it have made a difference to be reading a Jewish book? It wasn't forbidden to read the novel, after all. Even knowing that she shouldn't really be doing it, she was soon lost in her story.

There was a knock at the door. It had to be Michael. Jerry wouldn't have known that he should knock, he would have rung the bell.

She opened it to find Jerry and Richard standing there. She gave a sigh of relief. Jerry was wearing a suit and yarmulke and was looking quite respectable. She had to look twice at Richard to even recognize him.

He had cut his hair and he was also wearing a suit, but

there was something about him that looked very, very different. Whereas his eyes had always looked red, strained, and strange, they now held an openness and a clarity. He had changed!

Grandpa emerged from his room and peered at Richard. "Okay, my boy," he finally said. "You did it like you said you would," and he shook hands with him. "I knew you had it in you."

"I have you to thank for that," said Richard.

Jerry was looking somewhat confused.

"What did my son do?" he asked, not really expecting an answer. Instead he walked over to the bookcase and started examining the books.

"Hey," he said, "there are a whole lot of Jewish books in English. I thought they were all supposed to be in Hebrew. Actually, some of them don't look so bad at all."

He picked up a book, and was immediately absorbed in it.

"That's it," he said. "This sounds like me — lack of self-esteem — that's it." He turned the page to see who the author was. A doctor — a psychiatrist and a religious one. He had thought that only rabbis were really religious, and Michael and his family. A rabbi, yes; that was his job and therefore his family had to be *frum* as well. But surely no one expected the ordinary Jew in the street to eat kosher, to keep Shabbos. After all, who really did that?

"Can I borrow this?" he asked at last.

"Yes, but come pick it up tomorrow night," Sandy said. "We don't carry on Shabbos."

Jerry shot her an odd look, but put the book back on the shelf.

At that moment, Michael and the boys arrived back from *shul.* Jerry stared at them for a few seconds and then put out his hand to say "Good Shabbos."

"I do envy your family," he said. "You seem to have something so different — just to see you with your two sons."

"I see you with your son now," said Michael, smiling.

Jerry looked at Richard and suddenly seemed to swell with pride.

"My son, yes," he said. "I haven't really gone out with him before. I mean, not in this way. He really is a fine boy, isn't he?"

"Yes," said Grandpa. "I don't think you even know how fine."

Michael made Kiddush, and after washing for challah, the family sat down to a delicious meal.

Jerry ate as if he hadn't eaten for several weeks.

Richard was obviously quite at home with a Shabbos table. He must have been eating Shabbos meals somewhere, probably with the Rabbi, thought Michael. He remembered when his family used to go to the Rabbi for the full Shabbos and then for the Shabbos meals. Was that only three years ago? It seemed like an eternity.

Jerry kept asking questions, and Michael's whole family responded — explaining various aspects of Judaism. Jerry seemed to devour it just as hungrily as he did the food.

This is what a Shabbos table should really be like, Michael suddenly thought. A place with guests who are "hungry" for *Yiddishkeit* and for Shabbos, even though they themselves are not aware that they're hungry.

He felt a surge of enthusiasm that he hadn't felt for months. Maybe he should tell a story at the Shabbos table, as the Rabbi did.

He had always felt reluctant to do this, even with his own family, and definitely in front of his *frum* friends. He had only been *frum* himself for three years, so how could he know much? But he could respond to Jerry's complete lack of knowledge and his excitement at learning. His three years of being *frum* put him far ahead in his *Yiddishkeit*. After all, some university degrees took three years, and he was learning with the Rabbi now, every morning.

He thought for a few minutes and a story came into his mind, a beautiful *mashal* that they had learned just a few days ago.

He started to tell it and was surprised to see how his own family reacted — with interest and pride. He found himself giving some explanation of the *mashal* which he had come across in his own learning that the Rabbi had given him to do. It was received by everyone at the table like rain on parched ground.

This is really a Shabbos table, he thought, and he remembered how his Shabbos table had become over the years, with the children screaming at one another, and very little talk about anything to do with Shabbos except for the occasional Shabbos song.

He remembered rather guiltily that his son, Daniel, had desperately tried to change this. He had tried to prepare something *Shabbosdik* to speak about, but he had been good-naturedly shouted down, or listened to tolerantly until he had finished and they could resume their conversation.

Except for the children's friends, it was months since they had last had Shabbos guests.

He shivered slightly as the thought struck him that it was probably months since he had really invited "Shabbos" to his table. Tonight was different, very different. The *bentching* was done with enthusiasm and sounded very beautiful, and Michael noticed that Jerry and his son Richard both had rather good voices.

After Jerry and Richard left, arranging to go to *shul* with them the next morning and to return for the midday Shabbos meal, Sam and Dina approached their father excitedly.

"Let's always have Shabbos guests," they begged. "It was so lovely this week."

"We will," said Sandy, thoughtfully. "We will have Jerry and Richard, of course — but what about the Rozkys down the road? They always speak to me when I walk past. I think we should invite them for next week."

Her suggestion was met with wholehearted agreement.

CHAPTER 14

Michael gazed at the large, bright flame of the Havdalah candle for a few seconds longer before he extinguished it in the wine. This had been a very special Shabbos, a different Shabbos, something which he had almost forgotten about.

He decided that such Shabbosos should be repeated on a weekly basis.

He had almost forgotten about the weekday world, about his problems at work, but it was not long before the sickening feeling of depression overtook him again. How could he influence people to become *frum* when there was such a terrible shadow hanging over him? Who would listen to him if they considered him a thief?

But Jerry had listened to — no, hung on to — every word that Michael had said. In fact, he even said he admired Michael keeping his faith, even through this ordeal. What was it he had said, something he heard in the bar — about a man who spoke about Michael? It hadn't been someone from his branch of the bank. In fact, it seemed to be someone from a branch that had nothing to do with the accounts they were handling, someone only vaguely connected with theirs. At the same time, he seemed to have known quite a bit about the Selby firm, more than he should have known. Even Jerry had noticed that. Michael had not pursued this on Shabbos. He would look into it later.

Grandpa had also heard Jerry's story. He seemed very interested in this information and questioned Jerry quite closely about it. He emerged with a graphic description of the man and an assurance that these days you could barely miss him. But Michael had gone to help Sandy with something in the kitchen and hadn't really heard this part of the conversation, and when he came back, they were discussing something else; he hadn't thought about it again — until now.

If only there would be some solution to his problem! If only something would turn up to free him from the suspicion which clung to him.

Sandy noticed him looking miserable and her mood immediately altered. "I am sorry, Michael," she said. "You are thinking of work again. But on Monday you are going to see that other lawyer that Rabbi Sandler arranged for you. There must be *some* good lawyers. Can't we forget about it for a day at least?"

She saw her husband sink into a deeper dejection and decided this was not the way to handle things. She changed the subject. "Michael," she said, after a few minutes, "I think Jerry was really interested. I think that he really wants to be more *frum*."

Michael felt himself being dragged, partially, out of his dejected mood. "Yes," he said. "He asked me all kinds of questions. He's quite bright, that guy."

"He must be," Sandy said. "To keep his job even though he's often hours late. They must not want to lose him.

"I wonder what will happen with his marriage," she added. "I don't blame Elise for leaving him. He is drinking way too much."

"I know," Michael said. "But maybe we can talk to her or something."

"What would we say?" asked Sandy seriously. "Even though he wants to be more *frum*, he is still drinking. He could become a guy who puts on *tefillin* in the morning and comes home drunk and abusive every evening."

"But it shouldn't work like that," Michael said. "We will let him know that drinking and *Yiddishkeit* just don't go together — like taking drugs and *Yiddishkeit*. Richard found that out.

"I wonder what Richard feels about this," he added. "I'll speak to him about it in *shul* tomorrow."

His depression forgotten for the moment, Michael got up from his chair and helped Sandy do the *motza'ei Shabbos* clean-up.

"This was a good Shabbos," she said. "A real Shabbos."

They both looked startled as Grandpa walked in dressed, ready to go out. He had on one of the latest cut suits, a jacket with three buttons, which Daniel had said was essential these days. He also sported a kind of Russian hat which made him look quite elegant.

"Where are you going, Grandpa?" Sandy asked.

Grandpa smiled at her.

"For the past thirty years at least, no one has asked me

where I am going. Why now?"

"But...but Grandpa! I mean, when will you come back?"

He was enjoying this, thoroughly, and with a flourish he looked at his watch. "Oh, in the wee, early hours of the morning," he said, enjoying the look of consternation on his granddaughter's face. "Rest assured, you can always contact me if you are worried, or if you really need me," and he pointed to the cellphone that was clipped to his belt.

With that he was out the door, leaving Michael and Sandy slightly stunned.

"Shall I follow him?" Michael asked.

"I suppose not," Sandy said. "He has looked after himself all these years. But he doesn't really know anyone around here. Where could he be off to?

"He was on his phone just after Shabbos," Sandy continued. "I heard him. Maybe he arranged some meeting. But it was strange he didn't tell us. I mean, he hasn't done this before."

They busied themselves with the clean-up, with some help from the children, but couldn't put Grandpa out of their minds. Had he gone to a movie? Surely he would have told them. Why had he been so secretive about the whole thing?

CHAPTER 15

Grandpa had never had a drinking problem, but at one stage in his life, the bar had been central. It was during an especially vulnerable time, and he had felt the need to talk at length where there would always be a listening, if not necessarily sympathetic, ear. He himself had always been a good listener and he had, in turn, spent hours listening to whoever needed to speak.

And so the old man was familiar with the bar scene.

He knew, too, that there was no place which compared to a bar for gathering information. On a few occasions over the years he had, in fact, gone to a bar to gather information which was vital to him. No one had ever realized his true aim for he had carefully perfected his "bar manner."

When he entered the bar on that *motza'ei Shabbos*, he found a seat on the periphery of one of the larger, less cohesive-looking groups, and ordered a beer. He could not allow himself to drink too much or he was liable to miss a lot and even say things which he shouldn't say. There were occasions when that had happened, especially early on in his life. He had regrets about it to this day.

A somewhat overweight young man had become the center of attention. He had bought drinks for several of the people around him, and they were busy listening to his jokes. Grandpa sighed. The jokes were not really funny or even clever. It was clear the young man had to buy his audience.

He learned quickly that the man's name was William, his wife's name was Hilda, and he had no children.

For about twenty minutes, Grandpa hardly said a word, being careful only to laugh at every joke. William cracked another joke, and Grandpa laughed particularly loudly. William was hooked.

Half an hour later Grandpa was in earnest conversation with William, and it was not long before he had confided that he had just bought a laptop and asked William if he knew anything about computers.

William in fact worked with computers and knew a great deal about them.

This interested Grandpa very much. He soon realized that this man not only worked with computers, but that it was his greatest love. They spoke for some time about software programs, graphics, and Windows 95. They were soon discussing all kinds of ways to "beat" or "hack into" a system. William had obviously thought about it a great deal. Soon they were discussing the Internet and e-mail. Grandpa suddenly became very secretive, looking dramatically around to see if anyone was in earshot.

"There's a question I would like to ask you," he whispered. "I've written all kinds of things on my computer, stored on C drive. I'm even writing my memoirs, which I hope to publish one day."

William nodded, obviously bored. Was he going to have to hear all about these memoirs? But this was not what the old man was asking.

"Is it possible for anyone to get into my computer and read all my letters and memoirs?"

"It depends on who has access to the machine. Anyone can read anything if they sit at your computer, unless you use passwords and things."

But that was not what the old man was asking. "I don't mean someone getting in from my computer — I mean from a remote computer. Could someone somewhere on another computer get into mine and read everything?"

"I shouldn't worry about it, sir," said William, a little patronizing. "Who would want to get into your computer? Why should they look there?"

Grandpa stared at him. "That means," he said at last, "that means that it is possible."

"Only if you are connected," William said.

"But I am connected," Grandpa said. "I told you that." His attitude suddenly changed. "Hey, this is quite exciting. Is that what is known as hacking? Can people really do it?"

Grandpa looked at his watch. "It's getting late," he said. "I must go. But what I'm hearing is that all kinds of things can happen in someone's computer; even computer crime. I must come back and discuss it with you sometime."

Even though William would usually have found talking to an old man a little boring, they had been discussing his favorite subject.

"Don't go," he said. "Please don't go. I haven't had a discussion like this about computers for a long time. I was always interested in computer crime," he ended, a little lamely.

Grandpa thought carefully for a few minutes. Was William someone who could help? Did he have anything to do with Selby, other than a professional interest in computers? Well, what was there to lose? He had to have allies and he had to work fast.

"William," he said. "I like you. I wonder if you can help me."

William put his hand doubtfully in his pocket. "My wife will be mad," he said.

"No, I don't mean that," said Grandpa quickly. "I want you to help clear a friend's name, my grandson-in-law, in fact."

William was taken aback for a few seconds, but then a boyish sense of adventure showed in his eyes.

"Involving computers?" he asked.

"Yes, yes, very much so." And Grandpa proceeded to explain the situation.

For a few moments William was silent. "I'll work on it," he said finally. "Everyone in the field knows about it. My wife, Hilda, is in the bookclub and she heard all about it from there. I'll talk to some people. There's a guy who sometimes comes into the bar who's always talking about it. Maybe he can point to something. And," he added, "could you please get me a copy of that Selby printout?" His face had become red and he was breathing rapidly.

Grandpa was hesitant. Such a thing would involve Michael in a strong breach of confidentiality.

"Never mind," William said. "If you would just give me the dates when all this happened, I can get hold of the printout."

"You can?" asked Grandpa.

"There are ways," William said.

"Thanks," Grandpa said. "Is there anyone else over here who is into computers?"

"There are several people. I will talk to some for you, discreetly of course."

Could he be discreet? Grandpa thought that he could.

At that moment, he saw Jerry lurch into the bar. He had obviously been drinking somewhere else.

William noted Grandpa's look.

"Do you know him?" he asked.

"He's our next-door neighbor."

"A nice guy," said William. "A really nice guy, but he drinks a lot, and he changes when he drinks. It's surprising how someone can have a double personality like that. He's like two different people."

Jerry had noticed Grandpa and lurched over to him. "Hi! Grandpa! What are you doing here? I'm going to take you home."

Grandpa looked at his watch. Yes, it was getting late and his granddaughter would be worried, he was sure of that. Perhaps discretion was the best thing in this instance. And he had made some kind of start with William. He wondered if William could really help. Was he the kind of person he was looking for?

"I'm coming, Jerry," Grandpa said as he stood up. He shook hands with William and walked towards the door of the bar.

"By the way, Jerry, who was the guy who talked about my grandson-in-law?"

Jerry looked at him oddly. "I described him to you, didn't I? I come here, and there you are talking with him," he said, gesturing in William's direction. "But he actually wasn't the only one who seemed to know all about it. There was some-one else. Tall guy, very tall, with green eyes and black hair. You can't miss him."

He pulled a little roughly on Grandpa's arm. Grandpa walked a little unsteadily out of the bar, seeming to lean on Jerry's arm, but in fact supporting him.

It was about three hours after Grandpa had gone that his family heard singing outside and opened the door to find Grandpa and Jerry walking arm in arm up the pathway. They seemed to be very drunk, or rather, Jerry did.

Sandy wasn't so sure about Grandpa. As far as she knew, he had never had a drinking problem — but perhaps, occasionally, he took a few drinks too many.

"I brought your Grandpa home," Jerry said thickly. "Found him in the bar, talking to the guys."

He saw that Grandpa was going inside the house, and he turned back, not towards his house but obviously back towards the bar. His house was in darkness.

"Where is Richard?" Michael asked, a little sharply.

"Richard?" said Jerry in surprise. "He's probably with the Rabbi or some of his friends. He wouldn't tell me, I am sure. But he's all right. Don't worry about him!" And with that, he was gone.

They went back into the house to see Grandpa sitting in a chair, stone cold sober, paging through a book.

"Grandpa," began Sandy, "why were you at the bar?"

"Are you telling me, Sandy, that I can't take a drink occasionally?"

"But Grandpa, your stroke. You must take care of yourself."

"I feel very well," he said. "Haven't felt this good in years."

Sandy looked concerned. It just didn't seem right. Something was going on, but she couldn't even begin to think what it could be.

When Michael arrived home from *shul* Sunday morning he was surprised to find the whole family packed and ready to go. His children, who were holding a picnic lunch, informed him that everyone was going to Gold Reef City for the day.

Grandpa had his camera slung over his shoulder and was looking really enthusiastic. "I hadn't realized that you had a little piece of my own history only a few kilometers away. I was chatting with someone in the bar last night," Grandpa said, "and he mentioned this place. The children told me more about it early this morning, and I spoke to Sandy, and we decided that today would be the day."

"But it's always so crowded on Sunday," Michael said, not sharing the family's excitement.

"There's no other day that you can go with us, Dad," said his youngest son. "It wouldn't be the same without you." Despite himself, Michael smiled.

"All right," he said. "Just wait a few minutes until I change into something more comfortable. In the meantime you can all pack into the car. But put all that stuff in the trunk or it will be too crowded."

Laughing, the family piled into the car. They hadn't been

to Gold Reef City for several months, but when they did go they always enjoyed it.

It was built on the Crown Mines Site, which had yielded 1.4 million kilograms of gold in its time. Now no longer mincd, some imaginative entrepreneurs had built a full-scale reconstruction of pioneer Johannesburg.

"This was once very much a mining town," Grandpa pointed out, as they drove towards the outskirts of Johannesburg. "In fact, the whole area was just a digger camp. That's the only reason that Johannesburg ever came into existence. It was only about one hundred years ago that George Harrison, an Australian, literally stumbled on the Witwatersrand Reef, the world's richest natural treasure house. People rushed to it in their tens of thousands. And that is why we call the area Gauteng, meaning City of Gold.

"And it wasn't just a crazy gold rush," he continued. "There was real gold to be found, and in many places there still is. When people thought they had mined out a site, they went deeper and found lower, richer levels of gold. Of course, even though we didn't have mountains or sea like Cape Town, we had gold, and soon we became South Africa's largest city."

"I went down a mine at Gold Reef City," Daniel said. "Would you like to go, Grandpa?"

"Down a real mine?" asked Grandpa. "Yes, I would love to go. It has been a long time," he whispered to himself.

They were approaching Gold Reef City. "There's a helicopter!" called Daniel. "Dad, can we go in the helicopter... please...please...."

Dina and Sam pursed their lips. They had no intention of

going in a helicopter nor down a mine. They had firmly resolved to stay on the ground.

But Grandpa's eyes were sparkling. "That should be fun," he said. "I think I am going to enjoy this place. I really do."

"Grandpa," Dina said suddenly. "Do you think this place is sort of...I mean, sort of from your day? Like when you were a child?"

"I think so," Grandpa said. "Do they have penny-farthings?"

"What is that?"

"Old-fashioned bicycles we used to ride."

"Yes, Grandpa, they do. They have bicycles with a very large wheel in front and a tiny one at the back. You can ride them."

"Are you serious?" Grandpa asked. "They aren't just on exhibit?"

"No," Dina said. "I even tried to ride one myself. It was very difficult and Dad had to push me."

"Well, then, where are we going first?"

"The helicopter, Grandpa, the helicopter."

The family joined the line to ride in the helicopter. Grandpa was surprised that the line was so short until he saw the price, and then he understood. He insisted that the helicopter rides would be "on him."

Grandpa, Michael, and Daniel stepped gingerly into the helicopter. Sandy stayed behind with the children to watch everyone lift off into the sky. They had been told to stay well away from the propellers, and they needed no encouragement to obey, moving even further away as the propellers began to spin, producing a minor hurricane around them. The helicopter moved up, up, and up, lurching into the sky. Michael's stomach felt as if it had been left behind on earth. Grandpa was looking a little green and Daniel was surveying the fast disappearing ground. It was like being in a bubble because the sides were completely transparent. They could see Johannesburg far beneath them, and they excitedly pointed out specific sights they could see.

"There's the zoo lake and the zoo!" exclaimed Daniel. "If we were lower, we could see the elephants."

In response the pilot began to descend until the helicopter was so close to the ground that several elephants could be seen clearly.

"I didn't think you could fly this low," Grandpa said.

"Oh yes," said the pilot. "That is the beauty of the helicopter. You can fly at any height."

The time was up only too quickly, and the pilot prepared for landing.

"If you don't mind," Grandpa said. "I will pay extra to stay up longer."

The pilot soared once more into the sky and Johannesburg lay beneath them, a massive, concrete city. To the South was Soweto, another massive city. They could see the Magiliesberg Mountains fairly close on the western side, and to the north they could see the outline of Pretoria's Voortrekker Monument, bastion of an era that was passed.

"Do you do this every day?" Michael asked the pilot.

"No, it's only worth it on weekends and holidays, when there are a lot of people, unless someone orders me specially."

"You mean, you do private work as well?" Grandpa asked.

"Oh yes," said the man. "I mostly do small business trips, and occasionally, when the hospital helicopter has been busy, I have acted as an ambulance. I have done a couple of First Aid courses but I am not a paramedic, so I prefer to take one along if I have time."

"It must be so exciting to be flying all the time," Daniel exclaimed.

"Well," said the man, "in general I like it. But if there is a lot of flying to do it can become tiring, especially this kind of thing, going up and down, up and down, up and down."

"So you didn't mind my request to fly for a longer period?" Grandpa said.

"No, no, I didn't mind that at all. I'm happy to do it. It's less work and less fuel to keep flying around."

Daniel secretly hoped they would land soon. Though he would not have admitted it to anyone, he was a little tense watching the city far beneath him. Every time the helicopter lurched he felt he was going to hurtle through the glass, landing somewhere in the heart of Johannesburg.

Sandy and the children were waiting eagerly for their return. All three stepped out feeling somewhat relieved to be once more on solid ground.

"Wasn't that an unusually long trip?" Sandy asked, as they walked towards the entrance of Gold Reef City.

"Yes, Grandpa paid him extra," Daniel said.

"That was good of him," said Sandy. "I am sure you all enjoyed it, but I was getting a little nervous."

"So was I," admitted Daniel for the first time.

They had joined the line and were soon inside the gates of Gold Reef City.

"I can't believe it," Grandpa said noting the station, the full-sized train, and the surrounding buildings. "It's as if I have gone back in time to when I first arrived in South Africa." He looked nostalgically around and then spotted the penny-farthing bicycles.

"Hey," he said. Grandpa grabbed Daniel's hand and pulled him into the line to hire two bicycles.

"Anyone else want to go?" asked Sandy. There was no response to the offer.

Daniel wobbled terribly on his bicycle, and it took him quite some time to be able to control it. Grandpa, however, mounted it a little gingerly but was soon off, peddling away. People stopped and stared at him in amazement. Grandpa was quickly causing a sensation — and loving every minute of it.

People gathered to watch the elderly gentleman handling the penny-farthing with such ease, as if he had ridden one for years — until it dawned on them that at his age perhaps he had ridden one for years.

Together Grandpa and Daniel cycled down the road to the Lower Village. It was as if they had ridden into another world. There was a tea parlor, a life-size replica of the Theatre Royal, a reconstruction of an early brewery, a pub, and an old-fashioned newspaper office. There was a Chinese laundry, a tailor's shop, a cooperage, an apothecary (with modern pharmaceuticals inside), a stockbroker, and, of course, Gold Reef City Hotel.

"Grandpa," said Daniel. "Everything here is so...well...so

sort of old worldly."

"This was the world I grew up in," said Grandpa, obviously exuberated by the experience. "Where are the rest of the family?"

"I don't know," Daniel said. "I think it will take them a while to walk down here. After all, we came down pretty fast."

"Didn't we!" Grandpa declared, delighted.

Grandpa and great-grandson spent a leisurely time seeing the way the blacksmith used to work with metal long before heavy machinery had all but eliminated his profession.

They crossed the road to the newspaper office and admired the old printing machines. There were even old newspapers there, and Daniel gasped when he saw how low prices used to be for a suit or a box of homemade chocolates. He read the advertisements for several minutes while Grandpa became filled with nostalgia about some of the events he remembered. Daniel stood in a short line and was given a printer's plate with his name on it. Now he could stamp his name wherever he wanted.

When they emerged, they found Michael near the hotel looking in both directions. "I came to get you both," he said. "We are all going down the mine. Everyone else is in the line. You have been down a mine before, haven't you Grandpa?"

Grandpa was suddenly very serious. "Yes I have. It was many, many years ago.... It will be interesting to go again," he said, and then his usual enthusiasm returned. "Have you been down a mine, Daniel?"

"Yes, I have, Grandpa. But I would really love to go again."

"What did you like best?" Grandpa asked.

"Oh, the lift, or the cage, whatever they call it."

Again Grandpa's face became uncharacteristically serious, and Michael watched him, puzzled. "Grandpa, you don't have to go if you don't want to."

"They give you real hats," Daniel jumped in, "with lights on them, and large gumboots, and of course a big, waterproof coat."

"Good," Grandpa said. "We will go down then."

They started to walk beside their bicycles towards the upper city.

"You can ride if you want," Michael said.

"Up this hill?" remarked Grandpa. "You must be joking. I would never ride up a hill like this. One thing you learn with these particular bikes: when you get to a hill, get off and walk up. They don't have any fancy gears."

On the way up they passed the horse drawn omnibus. "Long time since I've seen one of those," said Grandpa, a note of longing in his voice.

"The thing about this city that I like," he said, "is that it isn't just a miniature city. The exhibits are so realistic that you can walk into them and be in another decade."

They reached the line. Sandy was way up at the front, and she breathed a sigh of relief when she saw them. "Sam decided he's going to go with you," she said. "Dina doesn't want to go, and of course Chani can't in her carriage, so we three are going to the Victorian Fun Fair on the train."

"We'll join you later," Michael said.

Grandpa handed his bike to Daniel, who took both of them back to the bike depot.

Grandpa, Michael, Sam, and Daniel were soon at the front of the line. They paid for their tickets and were led to a long room, to select mining gear. They even had long boots and hats to fit Sam and several other children who had been in the line.

"An unusual mine," Grandpa said laughing.

It was not long before they were following everyone else into the cage. They would ascend to the fifth level underground workings, far into the depths of the earth.

Grandpa seemed to tense up as he went in, and he held onto Sam's hand very tightly. Michael was not sure whether he was doing this to reassure himself or to reassure Sam. Grandpa was not usually afraid of anything, but his face was several shades paler than usual. They descended into the earth.

With a jolt they arrived at their destination, and Grandpa visibly relaxed when they got out. This was hundreds of meters below the surface — a totally different world. They had been put into groups before they entered the cage, and now a tour guide emerged who started to lead them along the eerie passages. "Whatever you do," said the guide, "don't lose sight of one another and don't wander down any path that is not marked. These mines are honeycombed with passages, and we don't want to lose any of you."

Sam instinctively moved closer to his father and people looked at one another as if gaining comfort from one another's presence.

"Hey, but there is gold there, I can see it," Daniel said, as he was shown the seams of the metal in the rock formation.

"Why is this mine out of use? Why don't they keep on mining here?"

"We might one day," answered the guide, who had often been asked this question. "It just isn't worth it right now. There are many thicker, richer seams on which we are concentrating our efforts."

"Is it some kind of 'fools' gold?" Michael asked, having heard of a metal that was almost worthless but which looked like gold.

"No, it's real," the man said.

"Look over there!" exclaimed Sam. "There is a miner digging."

"He is an actor," the guide said. "We employ him over the weekend to pose for us. He actually *is* a miner, this one, but over the weekend he is an actor." As if to show his skill the man placed his chisel close to the seam and tapped it with his hammer, at the same time presenting them all with a huge grin.

It was not long before they arrived back at the shaft. The cage was waiting for them. Grandpa again whitened and allowed everyone else to go in before him. As the cage moved upwards he kept his eyes fixed on a single point on one of the rails. He emerged first from the lift, with obvious relief.

"We also have a ticket for the Gold Pour," Michael said.

They all filed into a hall. A bar of solid gold was standing at the entrance door. "Pick this up and you can take it home," said a friendly guide at the door.

Michael tried and laughed when he realized it was impossible. Daniel and Sam spent a long time trying to even make it budge.

"How much does it weigh?" Grandpa asked.

"More than three hundred kilos," said the man.

"Is it solid gold?" Daniel asked.

"To be exact, it is 88% gold, 9% silver, and the other 3% is other minerals," said the man.

The hall filled up and small doors at the front opened to reveal a furnace. With long tongs, a man pulled out a white hot pot of molten gold and poured it into a brick mold, making a gold bar.

Grandpa looked around at the people watching with fascination. However, there was one man who stood out. He was watching the gold with a feverish intensity, smoldering with some emotion which made Grandpa's mouth go dry. Where had he seen that before?

It was almost six hours later that the family, exhausted but happy, got into their car to return home.

It was with a certain trepidation that the man checked his e-mail. There it was, the message he was dreading: Jip asking for more money, a whole lot more money. He was to arrange delivery through his bank, in cash, of course. He was on no account to follow this up, otherwise he would be *dealt* with.

Couldn't the guy give him a break? What would Martin say if he knew about this? Well, Martin had said enough already. He wasn't going to let Martin call him a "moron" again. But what was he going to do?

CHAPTER 16

As soon as he entered Mr. Arthur Corbin's office, he realized that this man was different. True, there was a certain atmosphere of order and sophistication, and the receptionist exuded efficiency. But these must surely have been to compensate for Mr. Corbin's apparent disorganization.

Many valiant attempts seemed to have been made to order the chaos of his desk and shelves. Obviously Mr. Corbin consciously or unconsciously resisted this. The result was an extra measure of chaos.

Somehow this only made Michael feel more at ease. It was totally unlike the impeccable neatness of Leonard Wilkinson and Partners.

The man himself inspired confidence. He must have been well into his sixties with an overabundance of salt and pepper hair, and large brown eyes with heavy, but not unpleasant, bags underneath and bushy eyebrows above. His eyes held a look of compassion and intellect. Could Michael trust him? True, he had been recommended by Rabbi Sandler. He had also been told that Mr. Corbin had a certain honesty that the judges respected. He had a reputation for hesitating to take on and defend a person who was totally and undeniably guilty. Would he judge Michael as guilty?

As he waited for the man to produce an empty file from somewhere underneath some 1995/1996 law books. Michael suddenly felt a wave of desolation. Would anyone ever believe him? How could he trust a lawyer who did not trust him?

The lawyer found his file and sat watching him for a few minutes. "You are very anxious and pretty depressed about all this, aren't you?" he said.

What was he, a psychiatrist? But the concern in his tone got through to Michael.

"Yes, I am," Michael said. "No one seems to believe me."

The man nodded.

"Tell me about it, all of it, right from the beginning."

Michael began. The man seemed to have all the time in the world. And, what is more, he was not writing things down. He didn't say a word as Michael told his story, just nodded occasionally.

Michael found himself telling him every single detail. When he had finished he felt as if he had poured out his soul.

"So you see, I blew it," he said. "I signed that statement."

"But you said that statement was the complete truth," noted the lawyer, a slight question in his tone.

"Of course it was, but apparently I shouldn't have signed it."

"No problem," said the lawyer. "We are sticking to the truth. It's always the best method, especially when a man is so obviously innocent."

Michael's sigh of relief seemed to come from deep inside him. "Thank you for believing me," he said.

"Well, it wasn't so difficult," said the lawyer. "One gets a feel for guilt and innocence, and you are clearly innocent. Though you will agree," he went on, "that not to report that you had found a discrepancy and started working on the figures was foolish. The kind of foolish thing...that innocent people sometimes do," he ended with a laugh.

"So you will take on my case?" asked Michael.

"Yes, yes, of course I will," Mr. Corbin said.

"Could you tell me what your fees are?" Michael asked nervously. The previous lawyer had charged him a small fortune just for one unsatisfactory consultation.

"Your wife's grandfather phoned me early this morning," said the lawyer. "We have come to an arrangement. The account has nothing to do with you. Is that all right?"

Michael breathed a half-guilty sigh of relief.

"I understand he can well afford it," continued the lawyer.

Michael frowned. He knew Grandpa had some money, but he had never thought of him as one who could "well afford" the services of the best lawyers.

"I have actually heard of your wife's grandfather," continued the lawyer, "but it was long before your time."

Despite Michael's anguish, his curiosity was piqued. "What did you hear about him?" he asked, somewhat guiltily. After all, this was a legal consultation, costing he didn't know how much, and here he was making conversation at Grandpa's expense.

"I would love to tell you the story," the lawyer said, "but..." He looked at his watch. "Okay, we have time. Perhaps you would like some coffee?"

"Thank you, but no," Michael said.

"Oh, yes, of course, you are a religious Jew. I can give you a soda and even a plastic cup to drink it in."

The lawyer rang through to reception. "I'm taking a break now," he said, "for around fifteen minutes or so."

"But your client," the receptionist said. "Is he still with you?"

"He'll spend the break with me," said the lawyer. "And we need a soda, and, of course, my coffee."

The receptionist sighed as she replaced the receiver. She had worked for two sets of lawyers before, and no one had been like Mr. Corbin, not in any way at all.

But she knew his reputation in court of being able to sum up a situation and present old evidence in an entirely new and brilliant way, often bringing the case to a most dramatic conclusion without having to add one bit of new evidence. Yes, she liked working for Mr. Corbin. No one else would have let her have four days off when her grandchild was ill, nor helped to pay the doctor's fees. He was different than the others, very different.

"I only realized who your grandfather was when I was speaking to him about you," Mr. Corbin said, putting far too much sugar into his coffee. "Actually, your grandfather is a bit of a detective, besides many other things." He paused, sipping his coffee with obvious delight. "This story goes back to early Johannesburg."

"Gold Reef City," whispered Michael.

"That's right," said the lawyer. "Although your grandfather had arrived in Cape Town and had worked there for some time, the gold in Johannesburg attracted him along with many other young men. True, there were diamonds being unearthed in the Cape and the Orange Free State, but the discovery of gold seemed to draw people like a magnet.

"As you probably know, Johannesburg was the center of the goldfields, and though your grandfather later left the city and went overseas, this was where he spent his early adulthood."

"I wasn't really aware of that," Michael said. "I thought he spent most of his time in Cape Town."

"Well, he ended up working in a gold mine. I don't think he was actually working underground but I think he had to go down sometimes.

"While he was working in one of the mines, there was a very serious accident. One of the cages in the lift shaft broke loose and hurtled down to the bottom at tremendous speed. Everyone in the cage was killed.

"Your grandfather had something to do with the investigation into the incident. They accused one of the mine managers of culpable homicide."

"But wasn't it an accident?" Michael asked.

"There was something very sinister about the whole thing," the lawyer said. "They suspected either negligence or foul play, because the brand new cable was already frayed.

"Your grandfather solved it all. It was one of the scandals of the year, of the decade in fact. Something to do with the looting of the mines."

"It wasn't an accident?" Michael asked. "You mean

someone killed all those men on purpose?"

"Gold does strange things to people," Mr. Corbin said. "Some people were smuggling out the gold they were working with. They didn't have such efficient security checks in those days. One of the workers found the men who were responsible and either threatened to report them or tried to blackmail them. It was never clear which. He was in the cage that dropped.

"The crime was well hidden, very well hidden. Your grandfather uncovered everything, and no one knows how he ever solved it. But they still speak about it down in the mines, and they say that the fear of the cage stayed with him his whole life. They also say he was able to recognize the final stage of Gold Fever or Gold Madness, where a person loses all sense of morality and decency in his craving for gold. He also developed some basic guidelines for mine security, and after that it became difficult to smuggle or steal even small particles of gold from the mines."

"Ah, now I understand," Michael said thoughtfully. "So Grandpa was once a kind of detective."

"Oh yes, your grandfather has done scores of things over the years, but a good investigator he certainly was."

"Perhaps he'll come up with something in my case," Michael said.

The lawyer agreed. "That would make things a whole lot easier."

"He's looking dreadful," Michelle said.

"Oh yes," answered Sally, instantly leaving her absorption in the computer. "Oh yes, he really is. Guilt must be weighing heavily upon him."

"There are some people in the office who think he isn't guilty," Michelle said. "Quite a few people."

"How could that be?" Sally said. "Everyone knows he did it. It's obvious."

"But that's just it," Michelle said. "I was listening to people talking at tea time. Several people think he's innocent. They think everything was done by a crime syndicate. He himself says he just typed in the numbers to work backwards and see what had been done."

"Who would want to work backwards?" asked Sally.

"It's a way of working things out. My brother was telling me that last night. He has some accounting experience so he knows."

"Does he know about Mr. Berman?"

"Oh yes, everyone knows. Everyone is talking about it."

"You see? That proves it," Sally said, indignantly returning to the computer. Of course he was a crook. Everyone could see that.

Michael looked out of his office window at the cars driving on the streets beneath him. They were small, like matchbox cars.

There's a person in each car, he thought. Each with his own thoughts, his joys and sorrows, concerns and worries. Each with the things that are important to him. He often wondered if he would like to switch places with one of them, to be a different person in a different life, having different worries and concerns.

How would he like to be Mr. Caldwin, for instance, driv-

ing around in the latest Merc, living in the luxury of Hough-
ton. Was Mr. Caldwin happy? It certainly seemed that he
should be. But then, who knows what goes on in the lives of
millionaires? Respected, yes. He was respected by everyone.
But his millions were probably not enough for him, as he
chose to put in several hours a day at the bank. That had
puzzled many. Possibly he was bored with the prospect of
retiring.

Michael let his mind wander along these lines for several minutes, and then he sprang back to the present. No, he
was Michael Berman. He had a lovely wife and four children.
He was *frum* and he wouldn't trade any of it for anything.
But one thing he would gladly give up: his job. He would give
up: his office and all the people in it, except, of course, for
Stephen. Stephen was different.

He again went through the fantasy of moving with his
family to another town, another city where he would begin
afresh — a new job, a new community, a new Rabbi, new
schools for the children —*frum* ones of course.

There was no real reason why he had to stay. There was
no firm evidence against him, otherwise they would have arrested him long ago.

But he didn't really want to leave his city. He had once
again grown close to the Rabbi. He liked the community, the
morning minyan, his neighbors. Why should he have to
move?

Still, he dreaded going to work each morning, just as he
had on that first terrible day when the suspicion was aimed
at him.

The office staff had begun to talk to him again, but with

a certain distance and a coldness. There was no more small talk. He had no idea what was going on in the office anymore, or in the lives of the personnel. Except, of course, Stephen. Michael felt a sudden pang of uneasiness.

Though Stephen was almost Michael's age, he had never married and had only recently confided to Michael that he had at last found someone. The only problem — and certainly it was a problem for her and her family — was that she was Jewish.

Michael had immediately felt himself torn in half. Of course he knew that a Jew may not marry a gentile. But he found himself sympathizing with his friend, for he really was fond of her.

Sensing Michael's hesitation, Stephen had questioned him on it. Michael hadn't wanted to tell him, but Stephen had pushed, and he told him at last what the halachic position was.

Stephen had looked immediately relieved. "Oh," he had said. "That explains so much about her reaction and her mother's reaction. It's not personal, it's just that I'm not Jewish."

The problem then seemed to hit him. "But there is some kind of solution, isn't there? I mean, there must be some way around it?"

Michael did not want to tell him that he could convert. He had just learned with the Rabbi that a true convert has a special *neshamah* which pushes him to become Jewish against all odds. One is supposed to discourage rather than encourage, until the person really shows if he is determined to embrace Judaism on every level and at any price.

He was pleased that Stephen did not push for an answer, but he knew he would have to give one soon. He had spoken to Rabbi Sandler, and the Rabbi had offered to speak to Stephen himself.

"I will put him off, though," the Rabbi had said. "I will discourage him completely."

He wondered how Stephen was getting along with the young woman. Eva, her name was. Probably Chava.

Stephen had also said that he had heard something, vaguely, from his mother, that they had a touch of Jewish blood in the family. On another occasion, however, when he had asked about this, she had looked at him blankly. When he saw her again, Stephen would find out about it.

Michael came away from the window and sat down by the computer terminal. He was once again working on figures from a multimillion rand construction company.

He flashed some figures onto the screen. Something didn't add up. There was something wrong with these numbers. He felt his mouth becoming dry, and his heart started to beat faster. Large amounts of money were apparently missing again.

"Stephen," he called. "Come and look at this. I am not going to touch this. Come and tell me what you think about it."

"Wh...What?" said Stephen, sitting down and looking at the figures. He frowned as he flashed various combinations of figures on the screen.

"There is something wrong here, Michael. Large amounts are missing, and it's the same kind of thing that happened before. What's going on over here?"

★ ★ ★

Grandpa was delighted. "I was waiting for that," he said. "He just had to do it again!"

Michael looked at him, puzzled. More money was missing and Grandpa was happy?

"Now we have something 'live' to work on," the old man said mysteriously. "We can begin to set a trap, and see who will fall in."

Michael shrugged, not really listening to what Grandpa was saying. He was still worried, desperately worried. He was afraid that something, somehow, might point again to him as the guilty one.

But why should it? He had done nothing, he argued with himself. Yet his anxiety grew. He dialed Mr. Corbin's number.

CHAPTER 17

I t's impossible, Mom. I can't take it anymore."

Sandy looked at her eldest son with despair. What could she say to him? The whole family was under strain.

"Your friends?" she questioned. "Are they behaving differently toward you?"

"At least they are all still speaking to me, but in a way they are different," he said bitterly. "Zevi Sandler is trying extra hard, but everyone is talking about me, I know. I see them talking together, and when I join them they get real quiet. I mean, the whole class say they believe Dad is innocent, but they all feel sorry for me, and I hate being felt sorry for. Why can't we find out who did it? Is anyone doing anything about it, other than Grandpa?"

"Grandpa?" she said quickly. "What is Grandpa doing about it?"

"Something with his laptop," he said. "He goes into the newsgroups about computers and computer security, and sometimes he even posts in."

"Posts in?" Sandy asked vaguely.

"When you write in something to the newsgroups it goes on the Internet. You can read it from all over the world."

"Grandpa is writing letters to all over the world?" she asked, horrified.

"Well, just notes, really. And anyway, I don't think anyone knows it's Grandpa. He just uses his e-mail address and people can contact him."

"And have people contacted him?"

"Oh yes, I know some have for sure. It's all about hacking into systems."

"These things are totally beyond me," she said with a sigh.

"Grandpa, can I play Tetris on your computer?" Dina looked at him appealingly. "I really will be careful."

"You can play later, my girl," Grandpa said. "I have work to do."

"On the computer, Grandpa?" she asked. "How can it be work if it's on a computer? Computers are for games."

"I have to find out something," said Grandpa, "do a bit of detective work. That's fun also."

"Will you be able to find out that my father isn't a thief?" she asked innocently.

"A thief?" he asked. "Who called your father a thief?"

"My friends," she said simply. "Lots of my school friends. They say he is probably going to jail. Is that true? Does jail take a long time? Will he be able to get kosher food?"

"Dina you mustn't say that," he said.

"But it isn't me who is saying it. It's my friends."

"How did it start? What did your friends say?"

"They said that my father is a big-time crook and that he stole a lot of people's money and he would go to jail."

"Who said that?"

"Everybody," she repeated. "My whole class."

"But who started it? Who brought the story to school?"

She was thoughtful, and he continued. "Did their parents tell them these things?"

"Oh no," she said, looking quite horrified. "Parents don't tell their children stuff like this. They would never do that. They just discuss things while we are playing and listening, and then we bring the latest news to school."

Grandpa gasped at the child's honesty and simple insight. What she said was obviously true. Parents did tend to discuss things as if their children were not there or not listening or even not able to understand. "Did they mention how it was supposed to have been done?" he asked.

"Oh yes, Gramps, it was with a computer. That is why I think you could fix it with yours." She looked at the laptop affectionately. "I'll play Tetris later if you are busy with that. Shall I leave you alone?"

"No, Dina, no, maybe you can help me...sit by me while I do this, I mean, seeing that you understand what I am actually trying to do. I just have to get into newsgroups and then...oh yes, Computer Security, that should give me something today, I am sure."

Grandpa and great-grandchild were soon peering at the titles on the screen. Security on the Net: several postings were there. That was what he needed to look at. These people were cagey in what they posted, never direct, but one could learn a great deal about what could happen on the Net or a computer attached to the Net.

"Hackers, crackers, sniffers," he muttered.

"What's that, Grandpa?" asked Dina. "You're not swearing are you, Grandpa?"

"Not really, my pet," he said. "Those are names for people who get into other people's programs and read them and sometimes even change them. They go through passwords and codes and all kinds of things."

"And they went into Daddy's computer?" she asked, her dark eyes fixed on the screen.

"Not exactly into his computer," he said slowly, "but something like that."

"Could someone be looking at your computer now?" she asked. "That would be a sniffer, wouldn't it?"

He stiffened. "That's a scary thought."

"Can they watch me play Tetris?"

"No, no they definitely can't," he said. "You wouldn't be connected to the Net if you were playing Tetris."

She gave a satisfied smile. "Good," she said. "That would be really awful. I'm not such a good player, you know."

He disconnected, went into Tetris, and pushed the laptop over to her. "Your game," he said. "And if you prefer, I won't watch you."

Right after supper, Grandpa again announced that he was going out.

Sandy became quite agitated. "Please don't go, Grandpa. I can't have you becoming like Jerry."

Grandpa smiled at her. "Don't worry," he said. "I just like the company. Not that I don't like yours," he added.

This time, as he entered the bar, he decided to sit alone. William wasn't there, and he didn't see any tall, green-eyed, black-haired man.

He ordered a beer and sat at a small table for two. He enjoyed looking around, and although he did not make it obvious, he was scrutinizing the people fairly closely.

A man came over to join him, asking if he minded, and very soon he was listening to him pour out his troubles about his wife, his children, and his boss.

Grandpa listened sympathetically, occasionally offering advice. Such things were important if one was to become accepted as part of the bar crowd. The man was chain smoking, and Grandpa noted that he smoked only half a cigarette before stubbing it out.

Eventually, feeling much better for the "chat," the man left to try and "sort things out."

Grandpa pushed his empty glass away, stood up a little shakily, and made his way to a young man who was staring morosely at the chair in front of him.

The man started as Grandpa pulled out the chair and prepared to sit in it. He seemed about to protest, but weakly acknowledged Grandpa's greeting and once more enveloped himself in his cloud of gloom.

"What's the problem?" Grandpa asked after a few minutes of silence. "A girl? You can find another one. Financial? You could always rob a bank," he laughed.

The man snarled at him. "What kind of jokes are you making?" he asked. "Is your name Martin?"

"No," Grandpa said, hoping the man would tell him more. "Who is Martin?"

"Oh, he's always talking about robbing banks. Never would do it, of course. No one who does it talks about it. Always talking to everyone about making millions. Haven't seen him around lately."

He sank once again into his morose withdrawal, refusing even to make eye contact with Grandpa. Soon Grandpa saw William enter the bar.

He went back to his original seat, and William joined him. Grandpa immediately handed him a sheet of paper on which were the dates of the Selby printouts.

"Thanks a lot," said William. "Haven't done much work today. I've been too busy working for you on this case."

Grandpa smiled. William went on.

"I went and saw that guy I mentioned to you and tried to strike up a conversation with him about computer crime. He didn't seem the slightest bit interested. In fact, he didn't really want to speak to me at all."

"What's his name?" Grandpa asked casually.

"Martin, Martin Greenfield," William said. "I spoke to some of the people he works with, though. He hasn't spoken to them for weeks about it. I asked who he used to speak to. Apparently he spent a lot of time with your grandson-in-law and also with someone else in that office, Stephen was his name, and Stephen is the one person he still speaks to. And of course, other people, but Stephen he speaks to a lot."

"Stephen," thought Grandpa. "Stephen." He was sure that was the name of Michael's best friend in the office. Could he be behaving so nicely towards Michael because he, himself, is guilty? Could he be the one who is "milking" the Selby account? Things were beginning to add up. But he was not one to jump to conclusions. He would continue investigating and see what he could discover.

His suspicions about his grandson-in-law's friend, however, were short-lived. He went to speak to him early the next morning and became entirely convinced that Stephen was not only innocent, but that he was doing everything in his power to prove Michael innocent. He seemed relieved that Grandpa and William were also working in this direction. Stephen had purposely made contact again with Martin, because he, too, had not known where else to look. But Martin had seemed to have lost his interest in computer crime. He was far more interested in fishing.

"Anyway," Grandpa said, "as someone in the bar was saying, a person who talks so much about it would hardly do it."

"But don't you see?" said Stephen. "It might work the other way around. While he was just thinking about it, he might have talked a lot about it. But once he put a plan into operation, he had no more need to talk."

"Could he really have done it?" Grandpa asked. "I mean, did he have access?"

"No, not really," Stephen said. "Maybe he is in it with someone else. In fact, if he is in it at all, he has to be in it with someone else. Maybe he was looking for a partner by speaking to all the guys in the computer field?"

"That makes sense," Grandpa said. "Perhaps, together, we could go over it very, very slowly. But you need to work now. I'll meet you some other time, not in my family's home.

I don't want Michael to know too much, and he will be here soon. I'll meet you in the bar. Have you got time?"

"I have some," said Stephen. "And this is important."

"And," Grandpa added, "I once saw a trap set for someone, and he fell right into it. This person will try once more at least."

"Sounds good," Stephen said. "I don't know what you have in mind, but I am right behind you."

And there is part of the trap that even you and William won't know about, thought Grandpa to himself.

"Oh, and Stephen," he said, "do you have an e-mail address?"

Stephen jotted down both his home and his office e-mail addresses and handed them to Grandpa.

"One more thing," said Grandpa. "Is it possible for you to get William's e-mail address for me? Perhaps you shouldn't say that I am asking for it. Or is there any way you can get it without asking him directly?"

Stephen nodded.

CHAPTER 18

Jerry sat gloomily in his living room, a glass of whisky in front of him.

Here he was, abandoned, completely abandoned, in his house. Abandoned by his wife and daughter, for whom he had slaved away for so many years. What was the meaning of it all?

He wanted to be *frum* like Michael, but he didn't even have a family to be *frum* with — only Richard, and where was Richard? Out, as usual. He had also deserted him. No one cared. No one really cared.

He took another few gulps from the glass in front of him, and his depression grew deeper. Was life really worthwhile? Who would miss him if he wasn't around? Would anyone even notice?

He had wanted to become *frum*, but he was sure it would never work. He had even been to speak to the Rabbi, but what had it helped? The Rabbi had spoken to him about *Yiddishkeit*, given him one or two practical things to do, invited him to a *shiur*, and told him to go to a doctor about his drinking.

How dare he! What was wrong with a guy having a few drinks? Especially when life dealt him such a raw deal. A doctor, huh? Did he think he was ill? But it was true, he hadn't really been feeling himself lately. It couldn't be his drinking, that always made him feel better. Maybe he did need a doctor. He hadn't been to his G.P. for years.

In the meantime, he would go to the bar — go and see some of his friends.

Jerry emerged from the doctor's office looking somewhat baffled. Perhaps someone had "tipped off" the doctor. After all, why should he have concentrated so much on his drinking habits? But he hadn't told anyone who his doctor was, or, in fact, that he was going to see him.

The doctor had told him he was concerned about his liver. That wasn't good. A guy had to watch his health. A liver was important...you only had one of them.

He remembered that as a teenager he had seen someone whose eyes were completely yellow and whose skin was sallow from liver damage. He didn't want to be like that!

But not to drink, at all, not even a little? How could he do that? His drinking wasn't a problem. But perhaps it was...to his health. It was a big decision. But what would he do instead? He would no longer be able to go to the bar. Who would speak to him? Where would he find friends?

This wasn't a simple decision. What would he do if he felt miserable or depressed? His wife wasn't even with him anymore. Perhaps she would come back. She had always hated his drinking, she really did, though he couldn't understand why. He always thought he was a nice, cheerful person when he was drinking. At least, most of the time. Or rather, sometimes. But he wouldn't stop just because she objected. Can't let a woman dominate you. But his liver? That was something else.

The doctor had given him a prescription to fill as soon as he made the decision to stop drinking. He was to take medication to stop the "shakes." Shakes! How could the doctor say he would have the shakes? He hardly ever shook, except sometimes in the morning, but a small drink would always remedy that.

But was alcohol really a problem? Could it be that he wasn't seeing things the way they were? He wished he could read something on the subject, do a bit of his own research. But there wasn't much he could read at home, not about alcohol, anyway. Hadn't Elise gotten some book for him once? If so, he was sure he had torn it to pieces and thrown it out long ago.

He sat back against the cushions of the chair. Where was he going? Where was life taking him? He wasn't a bad person, was he? He hadn't murdered or robbed a bank. He hadn't let down his family in any way, he really hadn't. He had provided them with a nice house, a massive garden, a swimming pool, the best furniture. What else could they possibly want? What else could one desire in life?

The answer to the question struck him immediately, and he shifted his mind from it. Well, perhaps he was an alcoholic, and if so, this was the end. What could he do about it? This was his destiny, his fate. He was an alcoholic and his liver was failing, and he would become ill and eventually die, and no one would be at his funeral. No one would even cry.

No one would miss him. His wife, Elise, would find someone else, someone who didn't have an "alcohol problem." She would get married again. The children would have another father, because he was useless. Hot tears coursed down his cheeks. What use were tears? There wasn't even anyone to see them.

He had no hope at all. What was the use of living? Maybe he should just end it all, just drink and drink until....

He must have lost consciousness because he awoke about two hours later with a blinding headache and a sick feeling in his stomach.

What had he been thinking about? Oh yes, his liver and his drinking. And he had wished he had something to read on the subject. But he didn't, did he?

He went to the bookcase of "never read books" and, somewhat unsteadily, stopped to read the titles. At the bottom right-hand corner he spied a thick blue book and, unbelievably, it really seemed to be about alcohol. Why hadn't he seen it before? First he needed some headache pills and maybe, yes, maybe another drink. Or perhaps some hot cocoa would be better. He was beginning to feel quite chilled. Now that he was on his own he would have to boil the kettle himself. Did no one at all care about him? Was there no one else in the world who cared?

Well, maybe there was someone: his next door neighbors. They had been incredibly decent even though everyone said that Michael was a big-time crook. He wouldn't believe that. And even if he did believe it, he was a good man nevertheless, and his family were special people.

Settled minutes later with the book, a cup of cocoa, and

half a cake which he had found in the fridge, he started to read. This wasn't a scholarly work on the abuse of alcohol. These were stories. But these stories were all about people and alcohol — people like himself, human beings from all walks of life. There were the educator, the doctor, the lawyer, the housewife, the businessman, all of whom found that their lives had become unmanageable because of alcohol. All of whom had managed to change their lives and stop drinking.

Well, he would read one or two of the stories. Perhaps he could learn something. Some of them looked interesting. Perhaps if they could do it, he could do it.... Jerry sat back in his chair. "I have now taken my last drink," he declared. "I am going to give up. I am never going to take another drink in my life...ever again."

He felt somewhat smug in his decision. What would his friends say? Surely they would be quite impressed with his tremendous willpower. Perhaps he should give lectures on how he had beaten the habit of drinking. There were many people with this problem. He met them so often at the bar. He was sure they would admire him greatly. But wouldn't he miss them if he never went to the bar again? How could he just let go of his friends like that? It would be disloyal.

Perhaps he could still go to the bar and just drink Coca Cola. Everyone would be so impressed. And he would have done it all on his own, not with the help of Alcoholics Anonymous or anything like that. You just had to take it one day at a time.

He stood up and then quickly sat down. He would most definitely stop drinking and stop drinking right away. But there were a few beers in the fridge, weren't there? Now how could he waste those? And he did have some whisky left. He couldn't just throw it away. It would be a terrible waste of money, and he really didn't like to waste money. He would just drink everything he could find in the house and tomorrow he would start taking it "one day at a time," because tomorrow would then be today and today would be yesterday and all forgotten, so what would be the difference if he carried on drinking today? He was drinking today already, so it wouldn't be a complete day anyway. He made his way to the fridge, and quickly drank himself into a stupor. Tomorrow he would wake up and everything would be different....

"Tomorrow" he did wake up and everything was, indeed, different. Where on earth was he? The bed was extremely uncomfortable. How did he get here? What time was it?

He looked at his watch. As he had expected, it was around 11 A.M. His eye caught the date. It was wrong. There must be something wrong with the battery. It was fully two days out of sync. It wasn't Thursday, it was Tuesday!

Where on earth was he? He was lying on a bed in a simply furnished room. He didn't recognize the room at all. He looked around, completely puzzled by his surroundings.

The monster caught his eye, and he broke out in a cold sweat. What was that in the corner? He could hardly describe it. All he knew was that he had to leave this place immediately. The thing was a large, purple, shapeless mass. But then it did seem to have a shape, a horrible eerie shape, and he could distinctly see those gleaming red eyes. He shuddered as his eyes focused on flashing talons that were ready to attack. He had to escape. He had to escape fast. He looked down at the floor, but realized he could not escape that way. The floor was crawling with oversized ants, which seemed to be more like frogs. One of them jumped onto the bed. He tried to ward it off but another one followed swiftly after.

He felt he couldn't take anymore when a massive spider fell from the roof onto the bed beside him, and he started to scream. Why was his voice so hoarse? His screams could hardly be heard, even by himself.

A young black man came in, and as he entered the animals disappeared. "Good morning, Jerry," said the man. "Are you feeling better?"

"Where...where am I?" asked Jerry, bewildered. "How did I get here?"

The young man smiled a pleasant smile. "You don't remember?" he asked.

"I don't remember anything," Jerry said. "I just went to sleep last night in my chair."

"What was last night?" asked the man.

"Monday night, of course." Did this man think he was stupid or something?

"It is Thursday today, Jerry," he said.

"It can't be, it..." Jerry stopped and looked again at his watch. It did say Thursday, didn't it.

"Where did Tuesday and Wednesday go?" Jerry asked.

"You have been here since Tuesday morning," the man said. "You were pretty drunk, and you were lying near one of the Soweto railway stations. I didn't think you were safe there, so I brought you home so that you could sleep it off."

"Have I been awake?" Jerry asked.

"Oh yes," he said. "We have had some good conversations. You told me all about your wife and your son and daughter, and how you are heartbroken because your wife has left you and that is why you are drinking, and your son is going to the Rabbi, and there is something wrong with your liver...."

He might have gone on and on, had not Jerry sat up in bed and given an ear-piercing scream. "There it is! There it is! That monster, but this time his head is only teeth and he is coming for me. Please help me, young man! What is your name?"

"Philip," said the man. "Philip Molefe. Jerry, I am worried about you. You are having the D.T.s. I thought you were going to have them this morning when you told me there were bats crawling all over you. I have to get you to a doctor."

The monster suddenly vanished.

"Where am I?" Jerry asked.

"You are in my house in Soweto. The schools are on holiday, and I'm not teaching so I have been spending my time at home working on my thesis for my Master's Degree. And I have been looking after you, of course. Now that you are back to yourself, is there really no one I can contact for you?"

"Michael Berman," Jerry said, "and my doctor. If you have a phone book I will give you his number. Tell him I want to stop drinking. Tell him I have the D.T.s and am having terrible hallucinations. Tell him I want to go to a rehab center. I will go now, right away." He spoke quickly before the monster reappeared, as if the decision could somehow ward it off.

Philip nodded. "I really am glad about that, Jerry. You mentioned something about that while you were talking in your sleep. You spoke a lot about it. I was really hoping that you meant it. My father used to drink — that is how I knew what to do. He got really bad, and my mother took all of us and left him. He was very down about it, and then his drinking got worse. But then he got involved with AA and he has been dry for ten years."

"Did...did your mother come back to him?" he asked as if his life depended on the answer.

"Yes, yes of course she did. They are still very happily married."

"Thank goodness," Jerry said.

"One of the things my father said to me," Philip added, "was that you can't do it alone. He had to do it with AA. To do it on one's own could lead to failure after failure."

"I can believe you," said Jerry.

A minute later he let out another wild, hoarse shriek. "There it is! It is coming to get me! This isn't a hallucination, it is real! Save me from it, Philip. Save me!"

Michael and Sandy were so delighted with the thought that Jerry might stop drinking that he became quite offended. Everyone kept implying his drinking was a problem. How could they? It was his liver. Couldn't they understand? His liver was a bit more sensitive than others', so he had to be careful with it.

He had spent several days in a private hospital and had been "dried out." Now the decision was his, to drink or not to drink. The hallucinations and his trip to Soweto had frightened him terribly. Maybe it wasn't only his liver. The doctors had put him in touch with AA. Maybe he would learn something there. Maybe he really did need them.

He spent the first evening out of the hospital with the Bermans and ended up playing Trivial Pursuit with Grandpa for several hours. This was the first night in many weeks that he had not spent in the bar, apart from the time spent in the hospital and at Philip's, of course.

And it hadn't been so bad.

He had made plans to finish his game with Grandpa on the following night.

Later that night Michael prepared himself to say the Shema before going to bed.

He was thinking about Jerry. It would be wonderful if he could stop drinking forever. Strange how even after his experience in Soweto he still couldn't see it as a real problem. It was as if he had a "blind spot" about it. To everyone else it was a glaring problem, but to him it was something "all the boys did."

He started to say the Shema, his thoughts still half dwelling on Jerry. Thank goodness he wasn't like that — blind to a problem. Or was he?

He stopped a minute and thought. He actually wasn't aware of any problems other than external ones. But how could that be? He always read *Tachanun* in a half-hearted way, feeling he hadn't really "sinned" in any way, not since becoming a *ba'al teshuvah* anyway. Not a big sin, in any case, and he wondered if perhaps he, too, was blind to certain things or excusing them. He remembered the *shiur* he had had with the Rabbi that morning. He had learned something about Shabbos that he hadn't actually known before, which meant he might have inadvertently transgressed. He felt very shocked about it, because he had been *frum* for three years and should have known.

The Rabbi had not seemed at all disturbed about it. He had explained that *Yiddishkeit* was something which was never static in a person's life. You had to be growing constantly, and a person who was truly learning and growing would learn new things all the time.

He had heard the Rabbi say that before, but this morning it had hit him like a new concept.

At a certain stage in becoming *frum*, he had felt that he had "arrived." He was keeping Shabbos, kashrus, *taharas hamishpachah*. He was davening and doing everything he should. But had he really changed anything since that time? Had he really learned anything new? He had to admit honestly that the answer was no.

The Rabbi had added that morning that he himself was learning new things in *halachah* and applying them constantly — and he had been *frum* from birth! Was he, Michael, becoming "stale" in his *Yiddishkeit*? Was he excusing himself for all his shortcomings?

Like Jerry?

CHAPTER 19

"Rabbi Sandler," Michael said, just after the morning minyan, "I know that everyone is talking about me. People don't trust me, even people I thought were good friends of mine. Maybe I am oversensitive, but I feel people are keeping their valuables away from me as if I might walk off with them. I don't think I can take it anymore."

"You have to take it one day at a time," said the Rabbi. "I know it is difficult. But it won't be for long. I'm sure something will come up to prove your innocence."

"How do you know?" Michael asked, studying the Rabbi. Surely he didn't really believe that. Surely he was just trying to reassure him.

"You must have *bitachon*, trust, in Hashem. For some reason, Hashem placed you in this position. It has to be for the good. And," he continued, "I have noticed that you are adding a depth to your *Yiddishkeit* that wasn't there before. I can see it in all kinds of ways. Other people are noticing it as well. They admire you and how you are able to be so calm and full of *emunah* against such odds."

"Calm!" exclaimed Michael. "If only you knew!"

"I do know," said the Rabbi. "Yet even so, you are coming across very strong...and calm," he added.

Michael was thoughtful. "What bothers me the most is the *chilul Hashem*."

"But that is not your fault."

"I know...but still."

"And you have lost weight, Michael," said the Rabbi. He had been noticing this for several weeks. "You have got to look after yourself."

Michael let out a sigh. "I feel I am letting down *Yiddishkeit*. How can I go around with a yarmulke when everyone thinks I am a thief?"

"Does everyone think that?"

"I'm not sure. But there is one woman in the office who is Jewish. I keep overhearing her talking to people about this terrible religious hypocrite, and she means me. Maybe it would be better if I weren't *frum*." His words were bitter.

"Michael, even if a person is a thief, Heaven forbid, he still has to keep the other 612 mitzvos. No matter what a person does, he is never free to say: 'If I did this, I have no right to be *frum*.' We have to do everything we can. *Yiddishkeit* isn't a cloak we can take on or off to impress or unimpress other people. It is something between ourselves and Hashem. A person has to stop doing what is wrong, not to stop fulfilling the Torah. That is never an option."

Michael suddenly remembered the fantasy he had once had about how anxious the Rabbi would become if he saw him eating in a *treif* restaurant, and he found himself telling Rabbi Sandler about it.

The Rabbi smiled. "That was, as you say, a fantasy."

"Yes," Michael said, relieved that the subject had come up between them. "And another thing I picture is being in court, and the judge is up in front, and everyone is around. And my wife is there, and...and you are there, Rabbi Sandler, you are always there."

"If you were ever called to court, I would be there," whispered the Rabbi.

"And I am in the dock," continued Michael. "It is so real I can even tell you what I am wearing."

"Are you wearing a yarmulke?"

"Yes, I am," Michael said. "And I feel people are shocked by that, that someone *frum* could do a thing like that.

"And the prosecutor is there, and my lawyer. And they are speaking before the judge, and I am hearing all sorts of evidence against me. It is as if my whole life is before that court. And then the judge becomes very solemn and he pronounces the sentence: I have been found guilty and I have to go to jail."

"You think about the jail as well?" the Rabbi asked.

Michael was silent for a few moments.

"Constantly," he said finally. "It haunts me all the time. I imagine all sorts of things. I keep thinking: Will they give me kosher food and will they let me have my *tefillin* and will they try to make me work on Shabbos?"

"And then?" asked the Rabbi softly.

"And then, I imagine that they refuse to give me kosher food and I slowly starve, and they don't let me keep Shabbos and I try to do so against all odds, and I..." He paused, embarrassed. "I'm sorry. This is all just my imagination. I don't know why I am telling you about it."

"I am sure the *mesiras nefesh* in your imagination is very precious to Hashem," said Rabbi Sandler. "But fortunately you are not in prison and you still look like you're starving. Don't you eat?"

"Not really," Michael said.

"Michael, nothing happens to us unless Hashem wills it. You have free choice to do good or bad. But the circumstances around you are sent by Hashem. You just have to have that kind of *bitachon* and trust that everything Hashem does is right and good and best for us. Sometimes we are put in the most painful situations, but that is where Hashem wants us to be. And in these situations, we must keep the Torah at all costs.

"And your body, Michael, is not your property. It belongs to Hashem and is lent to you for your stay in this world. You have to look after it."

Michael sighed. He knew what the Rabbi said was right, and both he and the Rabbi knew the answer as the Rabbi asked the next question.

"Has this test brought you closer to *Yiddishkeit*?"

Yes, yes, of course it had, and that made things meaningful. Michael's face suddenly cleared. "There's one thing I should share with you," he said. "For the past few months I have been thinking that the sparkle had gone from the community, that everyone's *Yiddishkeit* had become flat and dry and routine, and that *shul* services had no more inspiration. But I see now that it wasn't the *shul*; it wasn't everyone else. It was me who was feeling these things. I had allowed my *Yiddishkeit* to become routine, and therefore I thought I saw it everywhere else. Now it is completely different."

Stephen was looking very agitated when Michael arrived at work.

Was it the missing money? He'd left the situation entirely up to Stephen, feeling he couldn't handle it himself. Stephen had worked many hours on it and had, apparently, been in contact with others about it.

But it was not the figures bothering him today.

"Michael," he said. "I won't be seeing Eva again. I had a long talk with her last night, and though she is not all that religious, it's pretty clear to me that Eva will only marry a Jew.

"She said that I can go and speak to a Rabbi about converting, but in this I am entirely on my own, with no commitment on her part. And it takes a long time to convert. And Eva doesn't want to see me unless I am a Jew, unless I do convert. And she doesn't want me to convert because of her. It has to be something that comes from within myself. And I agree with her. I couldn't convert to another religion just for someone else.

"But maybe it's something more than that, this Jewish thing," Stephen went on. "I've always felt a certain kinship with Jews."

"Maybe you have some Jewish ancestors?" Michael asked.

"No, no, I don't think so." He was suddenly thoughtful. "It's just that the little I do know about Judaism sounds so logical. I mean, the belief in one God and everything. It makes things far more simple."

Michael smiled. "But what about Shabbos and keeping kosher and things like that. Can you see the logic of those?"

"Yes," Stephen said. "If that one God gave certain directions as to how to live, I would follow them even if I didn't understand them. I mean, He is the Creator and Builder and Constructor and Inventor of everything and everybody. If the designer of a complex computer program gave us a handbook, we would be very foolish not to follow it."

At the mention of a computer program Michael's spirits sank. If only he could find a solution to his problem.

Stephen noticed his change in attitude. "You know," he said, "someone might even have gotten into that program through the Internet."

Michael frowned. "How could that be? This is a closed system, isn't it?"

"It's supposed to be, but all you need is one administrative server to be online to the Internet for some kind of hacker or cracker to get into it."

"But what about firewalls and passwords and the Orange Book on security. There's software to keep out the hackers."

"And why do they need the software if it's impossible to get in? That Orange Book was wonderful until the Internet opened up world wide. Now there are problems. Students have been accessing their exam papers. People have accessed all kinds of top security files."

Michael just nodded, and Stephen changed the subject. "This Jewish thing," he said. "I must have a look at it. Not only because of Eva, but I think, Michael, partly because of you, and Raymond from school. There seems to be something in this Jewishness you all share."

An hour later, Stephen was dialing the number of Rabbi Sandler. Yes, they would meet the next evening...eight o'clock at the Rabbi's home.

Michael sat in front of his computer terminal.

Where would he be without Stephen?

Stephen had indicated that there would be further police investigations. He would not enjoy that. But perhaps this time they would come up with something constructive, something that would clear his name, so that life in the office could become normal once again.

But would it ever be? Even if his name was cleared, would he ever forgive everyone for thinking he was a thief? He would also have given such a person the benefit of the doubt, but he would have stayed clear of him, even if he had told himself he shouldn't. So what else could they be expected to do? He let out a deep groan. Stephen, who was coming back into his office, heard it.

"What's the matter, Michael?" he asked.

"I need a break, I need to go away, even for just a few days."

"Why don't you do that?" Stephen suggested. "You still have some days due. The Jewish holidays don't take up all your vacation leave. Go somewhere quiet, maybe even for a weekend."

"Well, with the kids it wouldn't exactly be quiet, and I would prefer not to go away over Shabbos because I would need to find a minyan, that is, ten men to daven with. It isn't really practical. It's just that it's such a strain being in a place like this where everyone looks at you with suspicion."

"I don't believe everyone feels that way," Stephen said. "They are just confused and don't know what to think."

"Well, everything points to me."

"But the police haven't made any arrests yet, have they? If everything pointed clearly to you, they would have arrested you. Look," Stephen continued, "somebody has been tampering with the accounting program and making a fortune out of it. The police might work slowly, but they will eventually come up with something, because they are prepared to wait and build up their evidence. They probably know a lot more than you realize, and none of it points to you because you had nothing to do with it.

"Also," Stephen said, "you're still working with large accounts and a great deal of money. If the people at the top really suspected you they would have put you to work on something else."

"That's true," conceded Michael. "But maybe they are just trying to catch me. Maybe they're watching very carefully to see if I try it again and something else turns up missing."

"Michael, don't be negative. Things have to work out."

"Are you sure you don't suspect me as well?" Michael suddenly looked very vulnerable.

"You need a break, Michael. You're even mistrusting me."

"I'm sorry," Michael said. "Sometimes I think everyone suspects me, even my family."

"You really do need a break," Stephen said. "You hardly eat a thing. You just nibble at the food you bring to work, and you probably do that at home, too."

"Probably," Michael said. "Even my wife's grandfather has been lecturing me about that."

Michael's thoughts turned to Grandpa. He had always admired the old man's spunk and determination. Maybe they could go away together.

Sandy was enthusiastic.

"Michael, we both know how much you need a change of scene, and Grandpa probably does, too."

"But I feel bad leaving you with the children," he said.

"We'll be fine. Grandpa is sure to take his cellular phone so I can always contact you."

As if on cue, Grandpa came into the room.

"We were thinking that perhaps you and Michael would like to go to the mountains for a few days, maybe even next week," Sandy said.

Grandpa broke into a smile. "Excellent idea," he said. "Are we going mountaineering?"

"Not exactly, Grandpa," said Sandy. "We just thought you and Michael could go for walks and unwind a little."

"Wonderful! What about the Drakensberg? I would really like to go there again. I love the wildlife there: porcupines, baboons, jackals, hares, and many many birds, and they have even seen leopards there, and of course, snakes."

"I hate snakes," said Sandy. "I am terrified of them."

"They aren't all poisonous," Grandpa said.

"I still hate them," she said with a shudder.

"Where do you want to stay, Grandpa?" Michael asked.

"We should try to be close to the Royal National Park."

"Yes," Grandpa said, beaming. "Is there a hotel in the Park?"

"Sure there is," Sandy said, as she paged through a guidebook she had found. "It's a big one with all the modern conveniences, and it's always full of tourists."

"No, no," Grandpa said. "Let's look for something quieter, something less like a city hotel."

"This looks good," she said. "It's near the Royal National Park, close to the Tugela River. It's a mountain lodge with an 'old world' atmosphere."

"But I suppose you can only get there by landrover," Michael observed.

"You don't need one," Sandy said. "It says here that you leave your car at the other hotel. There is transportation for all the people who are going to the higher mountains. They also come and pick you up from the lodge."

Grandpa took the book from Sandy and looked at it excitedly. He began to read:

"From the Royal National Park you can see the Amphitheatre — a rugged, vertical, curved mass of volcanic basalt about 1500 meters high, and about 4 km across as the crow flies."

"Why is it called the Royal National Park?" Sandy asked. "Does it say there?"

"Yes," said Grandpa. "Apparently the Park was visited by the British Royal Family in 1947 and was named because of that. It says the hotel there is very busy all the year round. Michael doesn't need that if he's looking to unwind. Let's stick to the lodge."

"I really don't know why I'm speaking to you." The woman looked anxiously at Sandy. "I really don't know. I know you aren't in my situation exactly, and you never will be, but at least you might understand...perhaps...perhaps because of the trouble you two are going through at the moment. It is so difficult to speak to someone who's life is flowing easily. They don't know at all what you are talking about. They sort of listen but they see you as a kind of object, maybe even an object of pity."

Sandy was surprised when Mrs. Wolfson approached her. She seemed to have everything this world could provide: an enormous house with an acre of garden, a sparkling pool, a billiard room, tennis courts, several lawns. Mr. Wolfson was known to have a prosperous and thriving business.

She wondered what problems the woman could be having. Did she have trouble with her sons? They seemed to be very nice boys. What could be worrying her? By this time she had invited her inside and both were seated in the living room.

"I'll make you some coffee," Sandy began, going through to the kitchen to switch on the kettle.

When she got back she was surprised to find Lynette Wolfson crying. Sitting down quietly, she waited, sure that the woman would soon tell her what was bothering her.

"My husband's business in going into liquidation," she began. "I only found out this morning. We stand to lose everything, everything we possess."

Sandy drew in her breath in surprise. She had not known what to expect, but she hadn't expected this. "I'm sorry," she said quietly. "Were you prepared for this?"

"No, I wasn't, not at all. It came to me as a complete surprise."

"Your husband hadn't discussed anything with you?"

"Not really. Only, about a month ago he said that something had been happening with the business, and at times when he thought they should have been making a profit, they seemed to be running at a loss. The amount they thought they could fall back on had somehow eroded. Last night he said that before he had been worth something, and now he was worth less than nothing.

"I tried to tell him that he was just as worthy as he was before, as a person, as a father. But he couldn't hear me. He can only see himself in terms of property and rands and dollars. I just can't seem to get through to him at all."

"I understand that," Sandy said thoughtfully.

"You see, I knew you would," said Lynette, "and I think your husband would understand my husband. You have all gone through something very difficult. Do you think he could speak to him?"

"Of course he could. I'm sure he could. But would your husband want him to?"

"I'll tell him I spoke to you. He'll be angry with me, but at the same time he'll be relieved. He has a lot of respect for you all. He has been admiring the way you have handled things. He says that he has never seen a family with such faith and inspiration. He keeps saying that Michael has been accused of all sorts of things, and yet you all carry on in your calm and serene way, knowing that in the end everything will be for the good."

Sandy stared at her. Why were people so convinced that

they were all taking it so well? What did people really think? What did they think of Michael? Some people seemed to think he was a crook, others seemed to think he was a *tzadik*.

What Lynette said next came as a further surprise.

"Actually, I just remembered my husband mentioning that he wanted to talk to Michael. I can't really remember what it was about. It was something to do with the business and the money and everything. Oh yes, that's it. He wanted to talk to Michael some time because he had suspicions that something was not quite on the level."

"What do you mean?" Sandy asked, her heart skipping a beat. Did he think that Michael had been involved in something shady?

If Lynette noticed Sandy's anxiety, she didn't show it.

"I am beginning to remember it all now. It was so late at night that we spoke about it, and I was so shocked and confused. But you see, that is why he's hesitant to speak to Michael. He feels someone set Michael up and had him accused of stealing. A hacker or whatever you call those computer experts who meddle in other people's systems. He thinks that maybe something like that is going on in his own business."

"He should really speak to Michael," said Sandy, puzzled.

"When could we come over?"

"Well, Michael is leaving early tomorrow morning for the Drakensberg with my grandfather. They arrive back late on Thursday night. How about *motza'ei Shabbos*, Saturday night, at around eight o'clock?"

"Splendid, we'll be there," she said. "I do think you could help us a great deal."

CHAPTER 20

This is really Gan Eden!" said Michael. He hadn't realized how much he needed the holiday.

They had parked their car at the hotel, and went up the mountain in a Jeep. A woman doctor, Dr. Wendy Carsile, was with them. She often came to the lodge, and she filled them in on the walks and climbs they could go on.

"We won't be able to really climb," Michael said. "Grandpa..."

"Michael, don't let me stop you. I insist you do some climbing. I can spend that time relaxing and reading at the lodge."

The drive was bumpy and longer than either of them thought it would be. They left behind anything that could be called a road and were now traversing a very rocky path which went through the trees and around the boulders. Above them was the splendor of the mountains. Below them was...paradise!

Grandpa was sitting bolt upright trying not to be shaken by every bump. He had been carrying on a polite conversation with the doctor, telling her details of his stroke that Michael had not known. He had really been ill. Michael wondered if it was all right that he was going on a holiday like this. But the doctor didn't seem concerned.

Eventually they reached the lodge, a little exhausted from the long drive from Johannesburg and then the bumpy mountain ride. It would be good to just lie down for an hour or so before supper.

They were shown to their room. The receptionist mentioned that they had put in a small fridge as requested to assist with their kosher diet, and they immediately put away the perishable foods.

Grandpa lay down on the bed. "You don't mind if I rest for a few minutes, do you?" he asked. "The journey was a bit tiring." The old man shut his eyes, and within a few minutes was breathing heavily and steadily.

Michael continued with the unpacking, placing Grandpa's laptop and cellular phone carefully on his bedside table. After hanging up the few clothes they had brought with them, he decided to investigate the food situation. Grandpa would surely want some coffee when he woke up.

He stacked the paper plates, cups, kettle, and hot plate together with the biscuits and the cakes and whatever else could go without refrigeration, and he looked back to survey his handiwork. The room was beginning to look as if they were camping out. He gave a sigh, hoping that Grandpa would understand that when you had to take your whole kitchen with you on holiday your room would not always look its best.

The lodge would serve dinner in just over two hours.

How good it would be to just sit back and relax and order what was on the menu.

He caught himself. He wouldn't exchange even the smallest aspect of *Yiddishkeit* for anything. And Sandy had prepared them with some really delicious things. But he still wondered how Grandpa would feel not going into the dining room.

Grandpa slept solidly for three hours. By that time Michael had arranged a mouthwatering meal of roast chicken, potato and other salads, and olives. Sandy had even slipped in some sachets of jelly-powder which he had dissolved into two cups.

"Everything smells so good," said Grandpa, opening his eyes. "Is it really supper time?"

They ate well and then went into the lounge to socialize and order a drink. Michael was surprised when Grandpa ordered a Coke.

"I thought you were drinking stronger stuff," he said. "I mean, back home you are always going to the bar."

Grandpa smiled, not really prepared to discuss it. "I feel like some Coke right now," he said simply.

As Michael took off his *tefillin* after davening the next morning, he saw Grandpa watching. "I've never really seen you do that," he said. "I mean I know you put on *tefillin* every day, at home or at *shul*, but you must do it very early before I get up. I used to do it, too, many many years ago. But not now," he continued as he saw Michael pick up the leather boxes. "Maybe one day, but not now."

They went on one of the simpler walks in the environs of the lodge and then a slightly longer one in the afternoon.

Grandpa insisted that it was no strain on him at all, but that night he confessed to being stiff. "I'm going to play on my computer tomorrow morning," he said. "Don't you want to go on a real climb?"

Feeling guilty, Michael arranged a climb for the following morning.

Grandpa and Michael had had a great deal of time to talk, and they learned a lot about each other. That night Grandpa told Michael more about his background. For some reason, he was finding that *Yiddishkeit* was once more pulling at him.

"It's the children," he said to Michael. "It's seeing your children following in your footsteps. Yours, Michael, is a religion that is alive. You can pass it on. You have the capacity."

Can I? thought Michael. Is my *Yiddishkeit* strong enough to pass on to my children? In the beginning, maybe yes, but now? With all the doubts and resentments he was having, was it still strong enough? Well, it was certainly getting stronger by the day.

"Watch out for snakes," said Thomas, a fellow hiker, as they moved further up the path. "I know someone who nearly got bitten on this trail. There are some lethal snakes around here, especially the rinkal and the puff adder. The berg adder can be found further up."

"They'll run away when they see me coming," laughed Michael, "and hear me. I'm not one of those expert climbers. I make a lot of noise."

"These things don't run away," Thomas said. "They just

keep on lying right where they are until some unfortunate person steps on them."

"Don't worry, I'll watch my step," Michael said. "I have to anyway. I'm hardly sure at times where to put my feet. Anyway, I'm following all of you. You would have to meet them first."

He followed, aware that he was slowing down the party, being far more out of shape than any of them. Sitting at a desk and in front of a computer all day was hardly exercise. Perhaps he should do some running when he got back, or start riding an exercise bicycle.

The view grew more and more magnificent as they climbed. He was getting thirsty, and he pulled out his water bottle and drank several mouthfuls. Water in the Drakensberg had a totally different taste. No wonder they sold it in bottles and people bought it so eagerly.

He realized that his party was disappearing around the ledge, and he decided to take a shortcut off the path to meet them. That way he would even be slightly ahead of them, and it wasn't too steep. In fact, it seemed to be better than the path, and he would only be off it for a few meters.

He started on his way, pausing to look back at the view. Way below he could see the rolling grasslands of the Royal National Park, a sanctuary for antelopes and birds. Further up were the lower mountain slopes, grassy and flowering. There were also rivulets and waterfalls with showers that shone in the sun like sparkling diamonds.

He walked a few short steps, lost in the scenery beneath. He could stand and look at it all day. He stepped backwards — and suddenly felt as if an electrical storm had exploded underneath his feet. He winced in pain as he felt fangs sink into his ankle. He knew it was a snake, and he knew it was a deadly one. But he couldn't tell which one it was. It looked charcoal grey with an impression of yellow, and, as he watched, half waiting for another attack, it coiled itself under a bush. He was filled with indescribable pain and a feeling of pure terror. He knew he had to look at that snake again, to be able to describe it when he reached medical attention, if he ever did. But then, there was a doctor there back at the lodge, wasn't there? Perhaps he could somehow reach her. Sweat was beginning to roll off him, and yet he was chilled from shock.

He was not aware that he had been screaming and that the rest of the party were running towards him. The tour leader was the first to get to him. His face was an angry red.

"You left the path!" he shouted. "You...I told everyone not to leave the path!"

"I've been bitten by a snake," said Michael, feeling he was going to pass out.

"We know that," said the man. "We heard you. You yelled it at the top of your voice."

"I don't remember," Michael said weakly. How long did he have to live? Would he be able to get back to the lodge?

The snake had disappeared and one of the men who seemed to know about snakes examined Michael's foot. "You've been bitten alright, twice," he said gravely. "This one is the worst. But only one fang went in. The other was stopped by the top of your running shoe. And this second bite doesn't seem to have much venom. What did the snake look like?"

"Charcoal grey," Michael said. "With some kind of markings and an impression of yellow." Was he going to die right here? His foot was in agony and was beginning to swell.

"Charcoal grey?" questioned the man. "We aren't really high enough here for a berg adder. It's more likely to be a puff adder. But that is yellow grey with a flattened head."

"It had a flattened head," whispered Michael.

"Maybe the snake was molting or something," said a woman who had been holding back tears. "Don't snakes change color during molting?"

"We have to get help," Thomas said, interrupting. "And fast. A puff adder is a killer," he added under his breath.

"It took us forty minutes to get here from the lodge," said the woman. Several people looked at their watches.

"Let me run back," Michael said, looking around wildly at the horrified group. "Let me run back. I want to get to that doctor as soon as possible. I want to get to a hospital. I don't want to wait here forty minutes till you get there and forty minutes till you get back. I could be...I could be..."

"Dead," said the woman, somewhat surprised at herself when she realized what she had said.

"Yes," said Michael, aware that he was shaking. His leg felt as if it were caught in a roll of barbed wire. "I would rather not be here. I am going back." Nausea threatened to overcome him as he stood up and started to stumble forward. He realized that his balance was becoming affected but he moved on, somehow reaching the path. His foot was becoming more swollen by the minute and his leg was beginning to puff up.

"I'll go with him," said Thomas. "I need two other men

in case we have to carry him." Several offered and Thomas chose two of them. Michael, afraid that if he stopped he would not be able to continue, made his way unsteadily down the path.

Kobus, a teenage boy and apparently a runner, offered to beat the party to it and make arrangements for Michael's arrival. Without even waiting for agreement, he was off along the path, quickly overtaking Michael, whose leg seemed to be growing by the minute.

"Quickly, quickly, Mr. Berman has been bitten by a puff adder. He'll be here soon, if he hasn't died along the path."

Hysterical, the young Kobus burst into the lodge lounge, causing Grandpa to jump up as he heard the news.

"Where is the doctor?" asked the boy. "Isn't there a doctor here?"

The boy was looking around frantically, and his eyes lighted on Grandpa. "It's your son, isn't it?" he asked. "You had better go to him. Is there a doctor here? There must be a doctor here."

"She's gone out for the day, to the National Park. She should be back in a couple of hours," said one of the guests. Almost in a trance, Grandpa moved towards the door. "How far away is he? How long will he take to get here?"

"Well, he was sort of hopping or hobbling, but he was going quite fast and his leg kept on swelling. Maybe the other three men are carrying him by now. Maybe he is unconscious."

Grandpa wished the boy would stop expressing his own fears. "My...er...son...was bitten?"

"Yes, by a puff adder. He was bitten twice. He is coming back. They were forty minutes away."

"How long did you take to get here young man?" asked Grandpa.

The boy looked at his watch. "About twenty minutes," he said. "I ran ahead so that people could get things ready."

"Get what ready?" asked Grandpa. "What does one do in such a situation? To be running or walking on a snakebite, doesn't it spread the poison?"

"They discussed that," said the boy. "They decided that if he was prepared to run or hobble along, they were prepared to go with him."

"Is there a hospital near here?" Grandpa asked the receptionist, who had come over to hear what Kobus was saying.

"There is a country hospital, not a big one, about fifty kilometers from here. They don't have much there, but at least they will have a doctor and some medications. We'll get a Jeep ready for him and take him immediately."

Grandpa moved to the door and looked out. Four men were approaching, one of them was Michael. He was walking fast but with great difficulty. As he got nearer, Grandpa noticed how pale he looked, with red blotches on his skin. His eyes were glassy and wild. They made their way into the lodge.

"Let's make him more comfortable," Grandpa said, trying to steady his voice. Michael's condition was obviously critical. He had heard enough about puff adders to know the bite was deadly. Grandpa wrapped his arms around Michael and felt his whole body trembling.

"We are going to the hospital," he said to Michael. "I am going with you."

"Have you told Sandy?" Michael asked. His vision was becoming blurred.

"No, I haven't," Grandpa said. "We haven't got time for that now. We have to get you to the hospital right away."

"Isn't there a doctor here?" Michael asked.

"Not at the moment," said one of the guests who had been standing around Michael. "She's gone out."

For a moment Michael looked as if he was going to break down. "She can't be out," he said. "The thought that she was here was the only thing that kept me going. The pain was so intense, but I kept telling myself that the doctor would know what to do."

"Then she fulfilled a good purpose," said Grandpa wisely.

Kobus, Thomas, and two other men carried a resigned Michael to the Jeep. "Hope your son is okay," said Kobus to Grandpa as he also hurried to the Jeep.

"I'm sure he will be," said Grandpa, patting Michael's arm.

"And sir, shouldn't you take some of your special Jewish food with you? You never know how long you will be in the hospital."

"A brilliant idea," whispered Grandpa and he rushed back into the lodge. Two minutes later he was back with some supplies from their room.

If the situation hadn't been so serious, Grandpa would have been enchanted with the little hospital nestling cozily among the trees beneath the mountains. There was a main building surrounded by prefabricated huts. The Jeep took them to the Casualty Department, which had lines of people waiting.

The nurse on duty acted quickly when she saw Michael's condition. The clothes around the bite had to be painfully removed, and he was changed into a hospital gown and put on a stretcher. The nurse made ominous clucking noises and amazed exclamations when she looked at the leg.

Then a young doctor appeared. He looked somewhat nervously at Michael's leg. "It is extremely swollen," he pronounced, quite unnecessarily.

"I know, I know," said Michael breathlessly. "And it is extremely painful." The leg was bruising badly, especially around the site of the bites, and it was hot to the touch.

"What does one generally do in a case like this?" asked Grandpa.

"Well," said the doctor, looking a little confused, "well...." He continued to examine Michael, checking his blood pressure, pulse rate, and lungs, and came once again to the leg. "You say it was a puff adder that bit you?"

"Yes, that's what the people said."

The doctor thought for several minutes, then went to a chart hanging on the wall. "His pulse is rapid and weak, and it seems to be a very bad case of peritonitis."

The doctor continued studying the chart. "I think the best thing we could give you now is an antibiotic. Penicillin would be the first choice." He went out of the room and came back with good news. "Well, I managed to locate an ampoule of penicillin in the hospital. I thought they had run out of it, but you are lucky...very lucky. I will see what else I can get for you. I will be with you soon."

"I should have asked him for something for the pain," Michael said. "I have never experienced this kind of pain before. It's as if my leg is on fire and about to burst, and my foot, and my ankle. Grandpa, what do you think is going to happen?"

"You are going to get better," Grandpa said, moving over to the chart and reading it. "What kind of hospital is this?" the old man asked.

"Oh, it is one of the country hospitals, probably with only one doctor who knows a bit of surgery. It's almost a third-world hospital. They are short-staffed and short of medical facilities and supplies. But at least there's a doctor."

"Could there be a phone here?" asked Grandpa.

"There must be," Michael said. "Or maybe your cell-phone would work here." Grandpa took it out of his pocket, but it indicated no signal in the area.

"I'll go and find a phone."

"You are going to phone Sandy, aren't you?"

"Sandy, yes. But first I want to get some first-world medicine for you."

"At least there is a doctor here," repeated Michael, as if this thought would shield him from any danger.

The nurse rushed into the room. "Sir, Mr. Berman, we are moving you into a private ward."

He was wheeled into a tiny room with a bed and a bedside cabinet, all in stark, but not really clean, white. Painfully he was eased out of the stretcher onto the bed, with an apology that the hospital was short on sheets, but that at least he had a bottom sheet. There had been a laundry strike earlier in the week.

"Is the doctor coming?" Michael asked. "I'm in a lot of pain, and I was supposed to receive an antibiotic."

"Don't worry, he has set that aside for you. He is just doing an emergency cesarean. Anyway, here is a bell; just ring it if you need us," the nurse said cheerfully.

"Before you go," Grandpa said, "do you have a telephone here? I think I saw one on the desk as I passed."

"Those phones don't go outside. They are just internal ones."

"Is there a main phone?" Grandpa asked slowly, feeling claustrophobic at not being able to make contact with the outside world.

"In the central office," the nurse said. "But it isn't open now. The administrative staff have all gone home, and they won't be here till tomorrow morning."

"But there must be some way to get to it," Grandpa insisted.

"Well you can ask the hospital matron," the nurse shrugged, looking doubtful. "But she isn't here at the moment."

"What happens in an emergency, a medical emergency?" Grandpa asked.

The nurse was becoming irritated. "We are totally equipped for all emergencies," she declared. "The doctor has already given me instructions about Mr. Berman. He is even ready to do an amputation." With that she went out of the room, leaving Grandpa and Michael in a state of shock.

Michael was becoming more and more desperate, and the pain was getting worse. The swelling had become more severe, and the leg was changing color. The nurse returned to take blood from Michael. She left the room without saying a word.

Grandpa stood up. "I am going to find a phone. Somehow I am going to find a phone."

Everything within Michael wanted to scream out that Grandpa should not leave him. But the logic of making contact with the outside world was obvious. If he were to survive, with his leg intact, he must leave this hospital and go to Johannesburg, or at least Durban.

Grandpa left, and the pain increased. Remembering that he hadn't even received his antibiotic, Michael rang the bell. There was no response. He rang again, and then a few minutes later again. It took him almost twenty minutes to realize that the bell didn't work. Its chord was frayed and brittle, and it probably hadn't worked for years. Did the staff know? How many people had died with their hands on the button of the bell ringing frantically for help, the staff coming in later only to cover them with a sheet, if in fact they had a sheet?

But he could call for help, couldn't he? He started to yell, his voice becoming louder and more frantic. Eventually, quite hoarse, he stopped, but the screaming went on and on. What was happening? Had his screams become living echoes? Perhaps the staff could hear these echoes and would respond to them. Had he gone mad?

And where was Grandpa?

It was an hour later when the nurse entered the room. "The bell doesn't work," he said quickly.

"Oh," she responded unhappily. "We have been very busy. There are many people out there, severely wounded people. There was an outbreak of fighting between Inkatha and ANC supporters, and the survivors have all come in. We have a lot of stab wounds and gunshot wounds — the doctor is busy stitching them up and taking out the bullets. The wounded from both sides are here, and we hope they won't make trouble."

Michael desperately hoped so, too.

"Grandpa, the man who was with me, did he find a phone?"

"He has gone," she said. "Someone offered to take him to a farm in the neighborhood. They have a party line telephone there. I hope he arrived safely," she added. "There was a lot of fighting on the road they were going to take, though of course we didn't know it at the time. I heard the road was impassable at one point. Perhaps it still is."

She turned to go.

"My antibiotic," he pleaded, "and the pain."

"We will attend to that," she said. "Don't worry, I discussed it with the doctor. He is ready to cut away the dead flesh from your leg, or even to amputate." She looked at the snakebite and the flesh around it, which was becoming suspiciously black.

By this time he was more aware of the screaming outside and the shouting and the crying, and he felt a pang of pity for the doctor. How could he, or anyone else, cope in a situation like this?

Again he was left alone with his fears and his despair and his overwhelming pain. Why had Hashem put him here? Why had he been bitten by a snake of all things? Well, he thought, he had been in Gan Eden, hadn't he? And who does one meet up with in Gan Eden...a serpent...and that snake seemed to have upset the pattern of the whole world. But then why did Hashem create snakes if they were so evil? Moshe in the desert had raised up a snake for the people to look up to and be healed. In fact, doctors still had this snake as their insignia. He had learned something about that, hadn't he? He had learned something with the Rabbi about that. Could he remember? Why was his mind so foggy? He realized he was becoming delirious from the toxins in his body. Would he lose his leg? What would happen to him?

Yes, he could remember now. Even the snake, so evil, could be elevated to a high level and become a source of healing and good. In the same way, everything seemingly bad could be and should be elevated and used for good. His mind turned to the office, where people thought he was a thief. Was there any way that could be good? His thinking was becoming more confused, but through it was a thread of meaning. Everything seemingly bad had to be elevated. And how could he elevate this experience, if he lived through it? Surely the poison was spreading through his leg, and it would have to be amputated.

No, he had to be positive. Hashem did things for a reason. Hashem didn't desert a person. Hashem was right here in this hospital. What could he gain from this experience? Perhaps it would make him more sensitive to the needs of others.

For what seemed like hours, these thoughts kept running though his mind. The hospital seemed to be quieter, and the nurse finally came in with his ampoule of penicillin. He was also given Omnipon, a potent pain killer which immediately relieved a lot of his pain. He began to feel better, but he wasn't better, and when the doctor came in he was quite agitated about his condition.

"Your blood," he said. "Your platelet count is extremely low. But I have found some antivenin for this particular snake. Giving snake serum is a risk, especially after so many hours. But I am going to try it."

Michael looked at him hopefully. This sounded good.

"I have to move you to High Care," he continued. "The danger of allergy and therefore anaphylactic shock is quite strong. We can't have you dying on us from the medicine," he said.

It took some time for him to be transferred, back on a stretcher and then back on a bed in High Care, this time with a top sheet.

There were eight other beds in High Care, most of them apparently occupied by victims of the fighting. Most had had operative procedures.

The doctor appeared and gave him a small dose of the medicine. He waited for a few minutes, saw that there was no adverse reaction, and then gave the rest. After a few more minutes he left the ward.

Michael lay back with a sense of relief. But as he lay there he found it was becoming difficult to breathe, as if he had to make a conscious effort to draw the air in and out. His muscles started to twitch, and he realized he was having an allergic reaction. His whole body started to convulse, and he was sure that this time he was going to die. Should he say Shema? *Vidui*? At this point he could concentrate on neither.

He felt as if someone were loading bricks onto his chest while he was trying to breathe under the crushing load. Consciousness ebbed away....

The doctor was not far away and was called immediately. He had had the Adrenalin prepared near Michael's bed in case of such a reaction. The nurse gave a large dose, but Michael had stopped breathing. They would have to work fast. The doctor worked with expertise, giving pulmonary resuscitation as he attached the electrodes to Michael's chest.

Both the doctor and nurse breathed sighs of relief as they saw color returning to Michael's face.

It was almost morning before Grandpa returned, flustered from his experience of being stuck in a ditch half the night and helping to place branches under the back wheels of the car until it could move again and take him to the coveted telephone.

His first call at around 2 A.M. had been to Rabbi Sandler, who had assessed the situation immediately.

"Don't phone anyone else until you hear from me," he said quickly.

Grandpa waited, gratefully accepting some coffee from the woman of the house.

It was barely twenty minutes later that the phone rang and Rabbi Sandler gave him the news. "I have been in contact with Dr. Levy, Michael's G.P. in Johannesburg. Everything is arranged for Michael to be admitted to the Linksfield Clinic over here: private, first-world medical care."

"But how?" asked Grandpa.

"The helicopter ambulance will be with you as soon as it is daylight. They have transported people from that hospital before. I want you to inform the doctor and the hospital so they have him ready. How is he?"

"He's not good," Grandpa said. "The leg is all black." The sound of the Rabbi's voice somehow made him want to cry. "Rabbi Sandler, please daven for him and say some *tehillim* for him. Hashem will hear you. You have a lot of influence over there."

"What about you doing the same thing, Grandpa."

"Yes, yes, I actually do remember some of the prayers." Grandpa found himself suddenly choked up. "And if Michael gets better, maybe I will start putting on *tefillin* again. It has been almost sixty-five years since I have worn *tefillin*."

"That will make a tremendous difference to Michael's condition," said the Rabbi.

"You know, Rabbi, maybe it will. Maybe Hashem will be so surprised to hear from me after all these years that Michael will recover."

"Please God," said the Rabbi.

CHAPTER 21

Michael remembered only snatches of the next two days. At times he was awake, but mostly he was asleep or tossing about in a delirium.

He remembered being taken to the helicopter and the noise of the engine as it rose from the ground, lurching its unsteady way into the sky. Two paramedics had been with him and, of course, Grandpa; they had tried to make him as comfortable as possible. The second dose of Omnipon had almost worn off, and his leg burned and ached and at times stabbed with pain.

He remembered being wheeled into the Linksfield Clinic and the initial relief of having arrived. Within an hour two specialists had seen him, and he had been given injections which made him lose contact with the world around him. He remembered Sandy's face and that of his older son, both looking strained and desperate with worry. He remembered the constant sound of *tehillim* being said by Rabbi Sandler and others, echoing and resounding through his brain.

His parents had come to see him, and they had watched him with a seriousness that had made him quite nervous. He had not heard the discussion that preceded their visit:

"The leg isn't very good, I'm afraid. It was a nasty bite from a deadly snake. At least we have him alive, though for many hours it has been touch and go."

Dr. Fischer of the Linksfield Clinic was discussing Michael's case with his parents, who had flown in from Port Elizabeth in the Cape as soon as they heard what had happened.

"We will try to save the leg, but I don't hold out much hope," the doctor said gravely. Michael's mother gasped. "But what will happen if you can't? How will he walk?"

"We can get a prosthesis fitted," said the doctor. "That is a false leg or a false part of the leg. It depends where we have to take the leg off. If we amputate only the foot or anywhere below the knee he is better off. He would learn to walk very quickly. The through-knee amputation is also not so bad. Above the knee we have a problem, but people have managed with that."

By now Mrs. Berman had burst into tears. "My son...he has always been so good. He is so religious, in fact, too religious. But why did this happen to him? Why did this happen to us?"

"We'll see what we can do," said Dr. Fischer. "He still has sensation right along the leg and even to the toes, and it is hot rather than cold to the touch. It is also navy blue rather than really black. At this point we wouldn't remove anything."

She dried her eyes. "Thank you, doctor. We will go and see him now. Oh...and doctor," she added as he was about to walk off and see another patient, "Doctor, please tell me, I got the impression that he nearly died in that country hospital in Natal. What happened there?"

"He was very very ill and, apparently, died clinically."

Her face whitened.

It was Friday when Michael finally came back to himself and was able to communicate properly with those around him. He had woken that morning with his foot throbbing. An injection had settled it, and he could relax and look around his room for the first time. He was in a private ward and surrounded by masses of flowers. The card on the arrangement nearest to him caught his eye. It wished him a speedy recovery and was signed by several members of his office staff.

That afternoon, they came to visit: Tom, one of the men who worked in the office, and Mrs. Jones, one of the partner's secretaries. They both looked somewhat embarrassed, and Michael related to them what had happened in the Drakensberg.

Mrs. Jones began, "We want to tell you, Mike, that we are sorry. I...I don't know what got into us. I don't know how we suspected you, and we just want to say we're sorry."

Tom muttered something similar and was silent. For one wild, brilliant moment Michael thought his name had been cleared, but then he realized this was not so.

This was a decision that these people had come to, prompted by something inside of themselves.

"What...what made you decide to tell me that?" Michael asked, not really sure if he wanted to know the answer.

By that time Mrs. Jones and Tom had been joined by another member of staff, Timothy, a young man who had only been with the firm for a few months. "Oh," he said, "we have been discussing it every tea time and we all came to this conclusion. It's just you, Mr. Berman, and your attitude, which made at least 75 percent of us feel this way, and we want to say we are sorry and that we were all really upset when we heard that you had been bitten by a puff adder, and we hope you will be well and that you will back with us soon."

"Apologies accepted," Michael said, and though he meant this, he was relieved when they went away. He wanted to be alone with his thoughts.

He was happy that 75 percent of the staff thought him innocent. But the thought of being the focal point of discussion at every tea break made him feel decidedly uncomfortable. And the other 25 percent who still suspected him? Who were they?

Well, he would soon find out, because if some of the staff kept their contact with him at several degrees below freezing point, he would know.

If only something would turn up to prove his innocence. If only!

Sandy came into the room, delighted to see Michael fully awake. She had sat for many hours at his bedside over the past couple of days, knowing that there were times when she had nearly lost him. The doctor had told her that he would recover and that even his leg was looking somewhat better. The possibility of amputation, however, had still not been shelved. They would know in the next few days.

Michael noticed the dark rings under her eyes. "Sandy, are you well? You look as if you haven't slept for days."

"What do you expect, Michael. I have been worried

about you. In fact I have hardly been able to do anything except worry and say *tehillim*. Grandpa has been incredible. He's been doing all sorts of things in the house I am sure he hasn't done for years just so that I can be free to be with you.

"And another thing," Sandy said. "Since he got back he has been putting on *tefillin* every morning. Did you tell him to do that?"

"We did discuss it a little, but he was far from putting them on. He actually knows an incredible amount about *Yiddishkeit*. He even remembers a lot of Gemara. While I was learning in the mountains he would look at what I was doing and make some comments directly related to the *sugya*."

"You're looking much better, Michael. The doctor says that even your leg is looking much better."

"It doesn't always feel that way," Michael said. "Did he say anything about...about...well...whether they were going to save it?"

"Apparently it is looking better even on that level. They don't know yet for certain."

"One time I was half asleep and half awake, and I heard my parents discussing what the doctor said. Believe me, what I heard terrified me."

Sandy could imagine what they were discussing. In fact the doctor had said something pretty similar to her.

She suddenly noticed the flowers from the office.

"They came to see me," said Michael, following her glance. "I don't know if it is just that they all feel sorry for me, but they were really nice and even apologized. I wish it was all over, though. I wish they would find out that I had nothing at all to do with it."

"Michael, let's not think about that now. We don't even know when you will go back to work. I am just so happy that you are alive, just so, so happy. Whatever the future holds, at least we will be together."

Michael continued to make progress over the next few hours. He insisted that it was too far for Sandy and the children to walk over on Shabbos. However, he very much wanted to make Havdalah for her and the children, and they decided that they would drive over right after Shabbos.

That *motza'ei Shabbos*, Sandy was in a rush to get to the hospital as soon as possible. "Grandpa, are you sure it's all right for you to look after Chanie? We could try and get a babysitter. I'm sure you would like to see Michael."

"You go with the other children," Grandpa said. "He will be delighted to see you after such a long Shabbos. Just give him my love."

Sandy quickly put together a few delicacies from the kitchen. In the hospital a person always felt hungry.

She stopped short, looking at Grandpa in consternation. "Oh, but what about Havdalah for you and Chanie? I never thought of that. I am just not thinking straight."

Grandpa laughed. "Chanie and I will sort it out. We have matches, candles, wine, and spices."

"But will you know what to..." she began.

"Sandy," he said, "I learned to say Havdalah many, many years before you were even thought of, before your mother was even thought of. As soon as Chanie wakes up we will make Havdalah."

Satisfied, she left for the hospital. She hoped Michael would be all right. Though he was now out of danger, there was still a strong question as to whether he would lose his foot or even his leg. Rabbi Sandler had made a "*mi shebei-rach*" for him in *shul* that morning. She trembled at the thought of what an amputation could mean.

Grandpa heard a cry from Chanie's room, and he went to get her from her crib.

He had promised to make Havdalah for them both, so he put together the spices, matches, candles, and wine, and found himself a Kiddush cup. Now he needed a Siddur. He did not really trust his memory, not after so many decades.

He had just got everything ready when there was a ring at the doorbell.

Mr. and Mrs. Wolfson were at the door, obviously having been invited over for the evening. Could Sandy have forgotten? Of course, with Michael's snake bite, everything else had just flown out of her mind.

Grandpa welcomed them in. "I am so glad you are here, Mr. and Mrs. ...er...sorry, I keep forgetting names. I suppose I am getting on. Sandy did tell me."

"Wolfson," Lynette said. "Bernard and Lynette."

"Sandy has gone to see Michael in the hospital. She will be back later."

"In the hospital!" Lynette exclaimed. "What happened? Why is he in the hospital?"

"Oh, a puff adder," continued Grandpa, picking up Chanie as she came to the door.

Bernard Wolfson stared at him in horror. "He was bitten by a snake?"

"Yes," Grandpa said. "On Tuesday morning. Please come

in and sit down and I can tell you about it," he said, noting that they were still standing uncertainly by the door. "I was there with him." They followed him into the lounge, Chanie delighted that there was company.

"We wouldn't have come," Lynette began.

"Oh, but you are here now and I would like to tell you all about it and we can eat a bit of..." he suddenly remembered that there were only five cookies left in the jar, "of supper, a Melave Malka. It will be my pleasure," said Grandpa. Yes, there was quite a lot left over from Shabbos. With a little touching up and some extra spicing, it would make quite a delicious meal.

He poured them each a drink and began to tell the story, stopping halfway as he remembered Havdalah. "Do you mind?" he said. "I was just about to make Havdalah when you came, the *berachah* for the end of Shabbos."

The guests stood respectfully while he said the words as if he had done so every week for years. Then he left them to be entertained by Chanie and busied himself in the kitchen.

When he came back in and continued his story, the most delicious aroma began to waft from the kitchen. No one knew that Grandpa was a good cook. He had made enough for Sandy and the children, knowing that they were likely to arrive back from the hospital hungry.

Mr. Wolfson started telling Grandpa about his liquidation. "That is one of the reasons I wanted to talk to Michael," Bernard explained. "I think we were framed by some sort of hacking into the system." Grandpa was suddenly alert.

"Framed?" he repeated.

"Well, I mean that my business got into this mess by

some skullduggery on the computer."

"Are you sure of that?" Grandpa asked, knowing that people tended to blame anything but themselves.

"I'm pretty sure," Bernard answered. He borrowed paper from Grandpa and tried to give a simple analysis of debits and credits. It did seem that there might have been irregularities, but Grandpa was struck by the clumsy way the man, a top businessman, was presenting it.

"Who exactly does these accounts?" asked Grandpa.

"Well, I had a young man working for me for years, but when he left I turned to a firm of accountants who looked after my books by an interlink computer system. I'm sure something's been going wrong there. I've seen all the printouts, but there is something missing, I know there is."

"Could you tell me the name of the firm?" Grandpa asked.

"Yes," Bernard said. "It's the Harvey Brothers. The actual Harvey Brothers died years ago, but the firm has kept their good name."

Did someone at the bar mention the Harvey Brothers, or was it Michael or Stephen who had mentioned it? Grandpa could not remember.

"Have you asked someone to investigate?" Grandpa asked.

"No," said Mr. Wolfson. "There is nothing to see. If it was done, it was done in an extremely clever way. You can't really notice anything. But I am sure someone hacked in somewhere."

"Excuse me, Bernard. May I ask you a personal question?"

"Certainly."

"Were you good at figures, I mean at school and all that?" Grandpa was being as tactful as he could.

His wife answered for him.

"Tell him, Bernard. There is nothing to be ashamed of. You are one of the cleverest and most creative people I know. But...Bernard, tell him about your number problem."

"Well, at school I had a terrible problem with numbers. But I do know enough to know that my business should have been running at a tremendous profit and not at a loss."

Grandpa was beginning to understand. The man was a sitting target for an unscrupulous hacker. "Could I have a look at your books?" he said. "I have run a few businesses and I would understand what is going on. Your secret is safe with me."

"Certainly," said Bernard. "I don't know how to thank you. And from what I can gather, what has been done to me is similar to what was done to the Selby Firm."

"Is it such public knowledge? Does everyone know?"

"Yes, I am afraid it is. Everyone knows what happened, and it points straight to Michael. In my case it points to me, not to make me into a thief, but to liquidate me completely."

"I think we should get on to it right away," said Grandpa, "but first we are going to enjoy a good meal," he said as he heard the key in the lock and knew the family had arrived back.

"I'm considering calling a psychiatrist in to see you, Mr. Berman. I think there are things that you need to discuss with him."

"Psychiatrist!" Michael nearly shot out of his bed but was quickly drawn back by the intense pain in his leg. "What do I need a psychiatrist for?"

"Well," said the doctor, "you talked a great deal while you were delirious. It seems you feel the police are after you, that you are being accused of terrible things. I mean, you are a religious man, a very religious man. Such thoughts must be...well..."

"Delusional?" suggested Michael.

"Delusional," agreed the doctor.

"If only that were so," Michael said. "I would give anything to wake up and discover that it was all in my imagination."

"You mean there *is* some truth in it?" the doctor asked, not sure if he should believe him. Surely it wasn't possible that this upright young man was a common thief. And yet — the doctor looked at his patient's clear eyes and intelligent face and shrugged.

"I'm sending you home tomorrow," he decided. "Of course, you must not walk on that leg for quite a while. We have a wheelchair to give you so you can get around."

"A wheelchair!" exclaimed Michael. "Won't I be able to walk at all?"

"Well," the doctor said, "you might be able to walk, with difficulty, but we don't want you to for at least three weeks. We are very happy with the way the foot has progressed. But there is still a great deal of swelling and bruising, and you can't play around with it."

"When will I be able to return to work?" Michael asked.

"After two or three weeks," the doctor said. "Perhaps by

then you'll be up on crutches."

"How long will I have to use the crutches?"

"Two or three months, I hope."

Michael gave a sigh.

"Don't complain, Mr. Berman. It's a miracle that you are going to be able to walk on your foot at all. It is a miracle that you are still with us."

It was good to be home, even though it was extremely difficult to get around. Michael had been told to rest and didn't need much encouragement. It was as if the puff adder had drained him of every last bit of energy.

Grandpa was continuing to try and clear Michael's name. No one was aware quite how hard he was working.

It was late. Surely it was time to shut down the computer and go to bed. Grandpa was the only one awake in the house. He had spent hours on the computer, trying to find out about breaking into other systems. He had learned a great deal and was becoming quite an expert. He had posted to many newsgroups, initiating all sorts of discussions on hacking.

But he had to admit that for all his time spent, he was no closer to the truth. There was still no way to pinpoint who the criminal was.

It was time to disconnect and shut down. He was about to switch off when a "Mail Received" message appeared across the screen. As he read the e-mail he realized that this was it, this was surely the key to clear Michael's name and solve the crime. The message was simple and unsigned:

```
Stop playing with these hackers. Some of
them can bleed you dry.
```

He hadn't thought of that, that there could be consequences and a price to pay. The chances were that the real criminal had used the advice of a hacker. If so, was the hacker asking for money? Was he hounding the thief? He would post back to this e-mail address, and possibly a few more. He would need to connect to a second server and use a second e-mail address, one that no one else knew about.

Stephen met Grandpa in the bar, as he did regularly. He looked upset, and Grandpa listened sympathetically to his problems concerning Eva.

"It will sort itself out," he said. "If you are meant for one another, nothing will be able to stand in your way. You are going to a very good Rabbi. Not that he would compromise Jewish law in the slightest way. But he will help you work it out, I am sure."

"William came to see me this afternoon," Stephen said, changing the subject. "He seems to have found several pointers towards Martin. He also brought me some of the other Selby printouts, in addition to the one we had originally. Then he brought me some of Martin's transactions. They don't seem to be totally correct. He could have been adding zeros."

"You mean that he was making tens into hundreds or thousands?"

"William thinks so."

"Where did he get the Selby printouts," Grandpa asked suddenly, "and Martin's?"

"I don't know," Stephen said. "He shouldn't really be able to do that, theoretically at any rate."

"Try to find out all you can about William as well, about his bank accounts, etc., can you?"

"I'm not sure," said Stephen. "But if he were drawing off money from an account, he wouldn't put it into his own account, would he?"

"Not unless he was in debt," Grandpa said. "He would settle his debts first, all of a sudden. Is there any way you could find that out?"

"Maybe I could phone and ask if his credit standing is all right for him to write out a large check, pretend I was a shop owner or something. I'll try something. But why should you suspect William? I thought he was working with us."

"I've thought all along that Martin had something to do with it, but there had to be someone else. Martin was obviously sounding out someone who would be willing to work with him, to do all the 'dirty' work," said Grandpa. "I also thought when the heat was on the other person would try and pull out and dump the whole thing on Martin. I..."

"Shh," Stephen said, suddenly. "There is Martin coming in."

Grandpa looked up to see a tall, good-looking bank teller with an almost babyish, innocent smile. "I will talk to him," he said.

Martin looked slightly uneasy as Grandpa drew a chair up next to him.

"I hear you are a 'boff' on computer crime," Grandpa said.

"I'm not really into it anymore," Martin replied distantly.

"Why? Have you already committed the perfect crime?"

Grandpa asked in a joking way.

Martin glared at him.

"There is someone claiming that, someone who perhaps doesn't like sharing the profits," Grandpa said.

"I don't know what you're talking about," he said.

"Perhaps it's just that he took your game of computer crime seriously and broke into a system, and is now blaming you," Grandpa said.

Martin looked at him with undisguised hatred. "Stop talking rot, old man," he said. "Go and prattle somewhere else."

With that Martin stood up and left the bar.

The next morning Grandpa received the phone call he was waiting for. William's bank manager had told Stephen that though his client had been in trouble in the past, his overdraft had been repaid, no more checks would be dishonored, and he was from now on an esteemed and trusted client. In fact, he had paid out massive amounts in cash on a fairly regular basis.

He had found out more than he bargained for, far more. An idea was burning itself into his mind. How could he test this? William had to have another e-mail address, and he had to find it out and post him an urgent message. But it had to be from some distance away. He had a friend in Hong Kong, a friend who wouldn't ask questions. Yes, the message should be posted from Hong Kong. That had a good ring to it.

What was it that had made him uncomfortable about William? Grandpa turned over in his mind all the dealings they had had.

Hadn't he suspected it ever since he had seen the young man buying drinks and telling jokes? This was obviously a young man who had suddenly "come into" money. It was too early in the month to be his salary.

Grandpa had spoken to him a lot. He wasn't a gambler, and he wasn't a person who was used to money. Certainly he was not a man who would naturally be buying drinks for the whole bar. It was the action of one not quite sure how to act as a rich man.

As Grandpa thought about William, he became more and more convinced — he would have to set a trap with Stephen's help.

It might be difficult. He might have to involve the police.

The man read the e-mail message with disgust. Jip was never, ever satisfied, was he? He had thought this last payment would keep him quiet forever. And here he was, using yet another e-mail number, this time from Hong Kong. Did Jip travel? What was he doing in Hong Kong?

His message was more threatening than usual. Would he never get rid of him? If he could find out who he was, he would already take some action of his own.

But Jip was clever, one of those geniuses who had turned to computer crime. And now he thought he had found a person he could milk dry of all the money he had managed to obtain.

Jip had to be silenced once and for all. Weakness hadn't worked. The more he had given him, the more he asked for. Strange that this time he hadn't even signed his name.

He reached out and poured himself another whisky. He

needed it, he was sure. After that he needed another. Now he felt his mind was clear enough to answer him. He began:

```
I have paid you enough. All you did was
to give me the software to break into a
system. I am sure you know exactly what
I have been doing with it with the Selby
and other companies. You could access
this yourself with your own software.
But I see you now for what you are. You
let everyone else commit the crimes us-
ing your software and then you milk them
heavily for it. I am after you now, Jip.
I will get you.
```

William clicked on an icon. It took exactly one second before it had disappeared from the screen to Hong Kong via cyberspace. The man poured himself another whisky, and another, and another.

CHAPTER 22

I'm concerned about Grandpa," Sandy said when Michael woke up to readjust the position of his leg. "He went out hours ago, and he hasn't come back. It's nearly 1 A.M. He's never this late."

"He's probably still in the bar, or following up some clue. He always tells us not to worry about him." Michael settled himself into a more comfortable position. "In the meanwhile, you need some sleep. He'll phone us if he needs us. He's a grown man, Sandy."

"But it was raining."

"Well, it's windy out but it doesn't seem to be raining now. Did you try his phone?"

"Yes, I did," Sandy said, far from satisfied. "I just got the usual recorded cellphone message about him being unavailable and please phone again."

"Well, he probably didn't have it in the recharger because of Shabbos. He'll phone us if he needs us."

Despite her anxiety, Sandy eventually fell asleep.

She woke again at 3 A.M. and tiptoed around the house to see if there were signs that Grandpa had come home. As she walked past his room, she saw through the open door that the bed had not been slept in and that there was no sign of Grandpa. Could he still be at the bar?

She looked through the telephone directory until she found the number of the bar. There was no reply.

She waited for ten minutes and then called the police, knowing that Grandpa would be furious if he knew. The police did not seem to take her seriously, especially when they heard he had gone to the bar. They reassured her that he had probably drunk too much and had been taken home by someone to sleep it off. They did agree, however, to check the area between the bar and the house to see that nothing had happened to him.

It was around 5 A.M. when the telephone rang. Sandy jumped to answer it. Could it be the police? Had they found Grandpa? Was he all right? Was he, Heaven forbid...?

Her heart was pounding as she lifted the receiver, and she almost cried with delight when she heard Grandpa's voice on the other end.

"Sandy," he whispered. "I don't want to be overheard. I was hijacked, or rather kidnapped, or maybe I was drunk and they brought me to a house somewhere. I don't know what happened or who did it, or maybe I did it myself. I can't remember. I just woke up. I don't remember anything."

"Where are you?" she asked, breathlessly, trying to hold back the tears.

"Well, I am in a room with a bed and a cupboard with nothing in it and..." Grandpa's voice seemed to fade into the distance. She was not surprised. The weather outside was terrible. She could hear the wind howling.

"Grandpa, where are you?" she asked as he came on again.

"Sandy, I honestly don't know. There is no way of knowing. The door is locked and the window is barred and open only about two inches at the top. There is no way I can get out, no way to find out where I am."

Sandy felt a sense of desperation. It was good that Grandpa had somehow managed to keep his cellphone. It was one of the smallest on the market so maybe it hadn't been noticed by his captors, if there were captors. He had obviously kept it off, which was why she had not been able to connect. Had he had time to switch it off when he realized he was in danger — if, in fact, he was in danger? Perhaps she could trace the call.

"Grandpa, how can I find you?"

"Impossible, poppet. I don't know where I am myself."

"But there must be some way. Here I am talking to you."

"That just means that I am in signal range of the cellular phone." There was a sudden gust of wind and again she couldn't hear.

"Poppet," he said, "I have to be careful of the batteries. They were already a little low last night when I left for the bar. They might start to wear down, and then I won't be able to contact you."

"Grandpa, I have an idea," Sandy said.

At that point, Michael woke up and heard Sandy talking to Grandpa. He sat up quickly, only to wince and lie back again.

"Grandpa," Sandy continued, "you can phone Vodocom — emergency number 112. Ask them to track you. See if they can tell where you are phoning from."

"That's a brilliant idea," Grandpa said. "I'll call them and then call you back.... Oh, and Sandy," he continued, "please do something for me. See if I have any e-mail and save it onto a disk for me, and put the disk away very carefully."

"But I don't know..."

"Daniel will help you. I have a feeling it is very important. Please do it right away."

Sandy replaced the receiver. At least Grandpa was all right. But where was he? How were they ever going to find him? She sat, watching the phone, waiting for Grandpa to ring back. How long would it take for Vodocom to trace him? How closely could they pinpoint a call?

After watching the phone for ten minutes, she was not able to tolerate the suspense and went to make herself a cup of coffee. Michael had once again fallen asleep. Time went on and on. It was already thirty minutes since she had last spoken to Grandpa. She dialed his number but again received the reply: "The number you have dialed is unavailable. Please call again later."

That was strange. Surely Grandpa would have left his phone on for Vodocom to trace and contact him. And surely as soon as he had been traced he would have called her back. She could not understand it. She could not understand it at all.

Suddenly Sandy remembered the computer. She didn't really know how to work it. Her knowledge of computers included little more than word processing and typing with three fingers. She went into Daniel's room. He was sound asleep, and she couldn't wake him. She thought to do it later, but remembered the urgency in Grandpa's voice.

She put the computer on the dining room table and switched it on. Windows 95 appeared on the screen and there was an e-mail icon. She clicked on it, found there was no new mail, and then realized that the computer was not connected. Well, she had seen Grandpa connect it up through the regular phone, and she did this. This time there was notice of four messages. Sandy knew she was blocking the phone for Grandpa to get through. She would have to be quick. But try as she might she could find no instructions as to how to save or extract the mail. Suddenly she saw the button on the computer "print document." She knew how to print — she had seen Grandpa do it onto his laser printer. She quickly got the printer and, somehow, ten minutes later she placed two pages containing the e-mail messages into her cupboard. When Daniel woke up he could save the originals to disk. She left the laptop on the dining room table so that she would remember to ask him.

It was 6:15 A.M. when she decided to call the police again. Their response was still unconcerned. "Your grandfather probably went to the bar and woke up in someone else's house after drinking too much. I am sure you will hear from him again very soon. If he is still missing in a few hours, call us back." However, the policeman had taken down all the details, opened a docket, and given a case number "just for the records."

Sandy began to feel desperate. Perhaps the police were right. Even Grandpa had suggested that he had been drinking too much and someone had taken him home and put him to bed. It had been 5 A.M. when he phoned, so no one in the house had been up. But why was the door locked? Perhaps, taking a drunken stranger into the house, it would be an understandable thing to lock him into a room. Or perhaps the door had just been very stiff and Grandpa had not been able to manage it.

She didn't mean to fall asleep again, but as she lay back on the pillows she somehow dozed off. She awakened with the sun streaming in through the curtains. Michael was already out of bed and was hobbling around the house trying to set up some breakfast for them all. The children were playing Monopoly on the floor, Sam and Dina being helplessly beaten by Daniel.

"Ma, please could you ask Grandpa if we can play with his laptop. It has a much better game of Monopoly."

"Grandpa slept out last night," Sandy said, not wanting to worry the children. "I left his laptop on the dining room table. He wants Daniel to save something for him from his e-mail."

"I don't feel like playing this on the computer," said Dina. "I want to play on a board. I want to throw real dice."

"That's fine by me," Daniel said. "I just thought you kids might stand a better chance against me on the computer."

Sandy left them with their game and went through to the kitchen to talk to Michael. "Grandpa isn't back," she said anxiously. "I can't even begin to imagine what has happened to him."

"But he phoned you early this morning, didn't he? Where was he phoning from?"

"That's the thing," Sandy said. "He didn't know."

Michael frowned at her. "He didn't know?"

"No. He just called from the cellphone. He was locked in a room with a bed and an empty cupboard. He had no idea where he was or who he was with."

"How did he get there?" asked Michael.

"He thinks he was kidnapped or something."

"But this isn't South America, this is South Africa. I'm sure he'll be back soon."

The telephone rang and Michael, who was next to it, answered. No, it wasn't Grandpa, it was Jerry phoning to confirm that he would be with them for the next Shabbos. He must have realized from Michael's tone that something was wrong. Michael told him about Grandpa.

Jerry was horrified. "But you have *got* to find him urgently. He's been hanging around with the oddest people in the bar, asking them all kinds of strange questions. If he is really on to something that they are trying to hide, they could do anything, absolutely anything. Apparently a great deal of money is involved."

"But why would they kidnap him?" Michael asked, beginning to take the matter seriously.

"To frighten him, to stop his investigations."

Michael started to worry. "I'll phone the police again," he said. "I think Sandy even has a case number, though the police have said that they won't do anything at this stage."

But he underestimated the South African Police Force. They had phoned Vodocom, given Grandpa's cell-number, and had been told that he had indeed called at 5:10 A.M. The call had been cut off by either the weather or a battery failure, but they had managed to establish that it was coming from the Boxburg area, East Rand, several kilometers outside of Johannesburg.

"Have you searched there?" Michael asked.

"Where should we look?" asked the policeman. "The man is indoors, somewhere, either locked up, as you suggest, or suffering from a hangover. If we were to patrol the streets, what would we be able to find? And which streets would we patrol? Boxburg is a very big area. We are waiting for another phone call."

"But perhaps the battery did go dead," Michael suggested. "That would explain Grandpa's silence."

"Vodocom were more inclined to believe it was the weather. The call was quite clear at first and then it just cut off."

Michael felt a cold fear grip him. Where was Grandpa?

When Grandpa had left the house for his usual evening at the bar, he was startled by the strong wind. Then the rain started.

At that moment, a car drew up alongside him and a dark-haired young woman leaned out and offered him a lift. He saw that there was a man sitting beside her and another one in the back seat of the car. There was another gust of wind, and when, in a cultured voice, the woman asked him where he was going, he pointed in the direction of the bar. The woman nodded, and he got into the car. The man in the back seat smiled and moved over to let him in. He was somewhat overweight, and he must have had a loose pin in his jacket, because Grandpa felt a sharp prick in his arm. Suddenly he felt unbearably sleepy.

He awoke around 4:30 A.M. in a strange bed. Where was he? He could remember nothing. Oh yes, it had been raining and someone had given him a lift in a car. Why was his head so heavy? Had he...overindulged in the bar? But he couldn't remember even having been in the bar. He couldn't remember it at all. But then, people did blank out with excessive drinking. Is that what had happened to him? Somehow, he had a feeling it wasn't.

No, his last memories were in a car next to a somewhat overweight man. He remembered the woman with the cultured accent and the long black hair. When he had gotten into the car he had not known her. Now he felt he somehow knew her better...surely her name was Jackie...and the two men.... Had he been with them all this time? Was he still with them?

He slowly got out of bed. Feeling somewhat dizzy, he switched on the light. Now he could see his surroundings. He was in a moderate sized bedroom with a bed, cupboard, chest of drawers, and bedside table. There were two doors. He tried one and found a small bathroom and shower.

Well, the other door must lead out of there. It was nearly 4:45 in the morning. He would have to be very quiet not to wake anyone up. But he would have to get home as soon as possible. He could imagine Sandy's panic. He hoped she hadn't noticed he was missing.

He tried the door. It was stiff, very stiff...no...the door was locked. For the first time he felt his pulse begin to race. Had these people kidnapped him? People didn't get kidnapped in South Africa, did they?

He walked over to the window and pulled the curtains.

There were bars on the windows.

Realizing that he was a prisoner, he sat on his bed with his head in his hands. What was the meaning of all this? What was he supposed to do now ? Should he wake up whoever was in the house? There must be some way of getting out of there, getting to some kind of phone.

Suddenly, he put his hand in his inside pocket. His phone was there.

It was important to call Sandy. She had to know he was all right. But what if someone came in? They would see the light was on and.... Before dialing he switched on the bathroom light, left the door open a little, and switched off the main light. Now he could see reasonably well, but he could not be seen. He saw that the bathroom had no window of its own.

His hands trembled a little as he dialed the number. He was relieved when he heard Sandy's voice on the other end of the line. They finished their conversation, and then he called Vodocom. He told them of his plight, and they asked him to hold on. After about five minutes the phone went completely dead. Obviously the battery. He stared at the phone for several seconds. There was no life in it, no life in it at all.

He could hear the wind whistling fiercely through the trees. Perhaps it was the weather that cut him off. But then the phone would have switched on even though he wouldn't have been able to connect.

He put the phone in "off" position and hid it deep in his pocket. Suddenly, he remembered the pinprick he had felt. It was the last thing he could remember. Had it perhaps been some sort of injection? Why should anyone want to drug him and kidnap him? Unless, he thought soberly, he was very, very close to the person or persons he was looking for. But then, why should they kidnap him? Why hadn't they killed him right away?

"It's true," Michael said. "There is no way that a police car could just drive around Boxburg looking at every house, without knowing the name or address. You would need a helicopter or something, and the police won't use a helicopter for this."

Daniel had been listening intently, his anxiety deepening as he realized that Grandpa was in real danger. "What about the Gold Reef City helicopter?" he asked. "Couldn't we use that? Didn't the guy say he hires it out?"

"That was for any day except Sunday," Michael said. "And today is Sunday."

"But it's so windy outside he probably won't be taking people up today," Daniel pointed out.

"That's true," Michael said, growing excited. "Can you find his card?"

"I think Grandpa had it," Daniel said. "Let me look in his room."

"Get his laptop on your way back," Sandy said. "There is something he wants you to do on it, so I left it on the dining room table."

"But it's not on the dining room table. Only the printer's there," Daniel answered. "I looked all over for it. You must have put it back in Grandpa's room."

"No," Sandy said, puzzled. "I know I left it on the table."

"Well, it isn't there now," Daniel said.

He went into Grandpa's room and came out again several minutes later with neither the computer nor the card.

"The laptop must be there," Sandy said. "Or maybe I left it in the lounge."

"What about the helicopter?" Michael asked. "You couldn't find the card anywhere?"

"No," Daniel said, "but we could always phone Gold Reef City."

Sandy phoned immediately and was told that the weather was not suitable for helicopter tours and they would have to wait until next Sunday. Feeling very doubtful that the pilot could in fact help them, Sandy took down the number. She dialed the pilot right away. He remembered Grandpa and was horrified to hear that he was missing.

"I can circle around," he told Sandy, "but unless there is some way to identify the house, there isn't much hope."

"At least we can try," Sandy said. "I really don't know what else to do."

Grandpa felt as if his head would burst. How long had he been sleeping? Why hadn't the children wakened him? They would have been up and about ages ago, especially Chanie, who always came to give him a hug in the morning.

Quickly, however, he realized he was still in the strange room, and he was a prisoner.

He went to the door and tried it. It was still locked. Should he shout to whoever was in the house to come let him out? He thought better of it, got back into bed, and lay back on the pillows. For some reason he was still very drowsy, and he half dozed, his mind filled with all kinds of confusing thoughts. What was this all about? Had he been deliberately kidnapped? If so, who wanted him? And what for? Surely it wasn't for money. That sort of thing was unusual in South Africa, and, anyway, he didn't have much money in this country, only the traveler's checks which he had brought. Of course, he could have obtained more on his gold credit card, but who was to know that?

Did this have something to do with the Selby printout? Had he found out enough to be a threat to someone, and, if so, to whom? There had been three people in that car so it was certainly not a one-man organization. Were they into bigger things than the Selby printout and the computer fraud from the other firm? Were they part of a whole gang of criminals?

He had suspected someone all along, but if that person was guilty, he was probably a small cog in a large machine. That meant that his life was in danger also, especially if he had made a mistake, as Grandpa suspected he had.

He wondered where he was. Everything seemed to be so quiet outside. Did he have neighbors? Would it be possible to shout for help to those neighbors? But it wasn't really so quiet. He could hear a throbbing sound of some kind of engine, and the sound was becoming louder and louder. With a start he realized that it was a helicopter, and almost instinctively he went over to the window to watch it. He was only able to open it slightly, and he shivered as a particularly vicious blast of wind hit him. He looked up towards the sky. Yes, the helicopter was fairly low, and he could see it quite clearly. It was very similar to the Gold Reef City helicopter. In fact, if it wasn't a Sunday morning, when the helicopter would be busy taking people for rides, he would have been sure that the blue and gold markings were the same.

Slowly it dawned on him that perhaps the weather had been too bad at Gold Reef City for the helicopter to be able to take passengers. Perhaps his family had hired it, and *perhaps* Vodocom had traced him to a certain area, and *perhaps* they had come to look for him. But how on earth would they find him? How was he to signal them?

He sat down on the bed and thought. A smoke signal? There were no matches, and what could he burn?

Ah yes! That was it! Whipping the bottom sheet off his bed, he held it out the window, breathing a sigh of relief as the wind caught it and billowed it out. But the sound was becoming fainter — the helicopter was moving off in another direction. Grandpa began to recite whatever *tehillim* he could remember.

"I think it's useless," Sandy sighed. "All the streets and houses look the same."

"There's the Bunny Park," Daniel said. "Maybe he is close by there."

"He wouldn't be able to call us even if he were," Sandy said despondently. They had been circling and finding nothing, and she suggested they call off the search, go home, and contact the police again. The pilot insisted on doing the complete route just one more time, even the outlying areas they had circled the first time. Sandy was beginning to feel somewhat ill as the helicopter rocked violently in the wind.

Suddenly, they made a sharp turn. The pilot had spotted something, something that looked like a massive white flag, billowing in the wind. Using the two-way radio in the helicopter, he was soon giving the police directions to the house, describing its location as precisely as he could. He had completed this even before Sandy and Daniel noticed what he saw.

"What do you mean?" Sandy asked, after he had finished his rather cryptic radio signal.

"What I just said — look over there."

It was unmistakable. Someone was trying to signal to the helicopter. Who else could it be?

It was about forty minutes later that Grandpa was brought to the Boxburg police station, where Sandy and Daniel were waiting. The pilot had waited to hear that Grandpa was in good health before moving off. He had insisted that he did not want to be paid. But Grandpa would make sure to take care of that himself. They had phoned Rabbi Sandler, who would be coming to get them when they were ready.

"I have no idea who it was," Grandpa said when they had been together for a few minutes. "No one was in the house with me. Of course, the police can quickly check out who owns it. The thing is," he said, shaking his head in a puzzled way, "I feel as if I have been to all kinds of places. I've had all kinds of strange dreams which I can't remember, dreams with mixed up times and places."

"We are taking you home and putting you straight to bed, Grandpa. You need some rest."

"You forget," Grandpa said, "I just had an overdose of that."

"I want you to tell us all about it."

"But I have no memory of it. If only I could remember. In the meanwhile, I am starving. I hope you have a good breakfast and lunch waiting for me."

CHAPTER 23

Sandy gave a groan. Purim had passed and Pesach was soon approaching. Pesach, the time of our freedom. "Well," she thought, "it will be a kind of freedom after spending the next three weeks doing Pesach cleaning."

She had halfheartedly started working on the house before Purim, but if she carried on at that pace, she might only be ready for Shavuos. She had to create in herself a "balance of panic": to panic enough to motivate herself to work constantly and hard, but not enough to paralyze her with anxiety.

Here begin the weeks of "slavery," the endless search for *chametz*. She would have to switch her mind into Pesach operation and think of nothing else. She was just about to tackle the hall cupboard when Dina and Sam walked in, holding very crumbly pieces of cake which they had cut for themselves in the kitchen.

"Did I say you could take that?" she asked, realizing that she had suddenly developed the very crumb phobia necessary for Pesach cleaning.

The children looked at her in surprise. "We usually take cookies, and you don't say anything, and this was in the same tin."

Dina licked her fingers, and a large crumb fell to the floor, which she proceeded to stand on, grinding it into the carpet.

"Don't do that," said Sandy with great control. "It is nearly Pesach."

"Pesach!" Sam said excitedly. "Pesach! We want to help!"

"Help?" Sandy was about to refuse, but stopped. She knew she didn't give the children enough responsibility, and here they were asking for it.

"Good," she said. "Clear up all these crumbs and then we can start on the cupboard."

To her surprise the cake was quickly put away and the crumbs quite expertly cleaned up. Their help actually made a difference to the Pesach cleaning.

There was a ring at the door and Jerry came in. "I came to see Michael," he said. "I haven't seen him for several days."

"He's back at work," Sandy said. "He started yesterday."

"Really? The last time I saw his leg it was still blue and swollen."

"The doctors insisted on a wheelchair. But his leg is looking much better, and he's in less pain."

"And how was going back to the office?" Jerry asked, aware of what it meant to Michael to return.

"I think most people were very friendly to him," Sandy said. "They already were visiting him here. There's one receptionist who upsets him, though. She said that the puff adder was an instrument of divine judgment to punish a criminal."

Jerry was shocked. "She said that to him?"

"No, but she said it loud enough for him to hear. I hope this case is solved soon."

"Please God," Jerry said.

"But tell me, Jerry, how are you?"

"I miss my wife and family terribly," he said. Both Michael and Sandy had noticed that he had become a different Jerry over the past few weeks. He had stopped drinking and was attending AA meetings regularly, and his behavior and health had immediately begun to improve. In fact, he looked years younger.

He was becoming involved with *Yiddishkeit* slowly but steadily and had built up a close relationship with his son.

He had never gotten over his wife, however. She had not yet divorced him, though she was now in touch with lawyers. Several people had tried to speak to her, even the Rabbi, but to no avail. She had heard that Jerry stopped drinking, and she had said, with a certain bitterness, that it would be good for him to make a new start.

Tanya, who had always loved her father, tried to intervene, but her words fell on deaf ears. Her mother absolutely refused to see Jerry and put the phone down every time he tried to make contact with her.

Richard had been to visit his mother several times, and she had welcomed him, but he was not allowed to speak of his father. There was to be a divorce and a *get*, and that was that!

"One thing I have decided," Jerry said. "Even if Elise divorces me, I am not going to give her a *get*."

"But you can't do that!" Sandy said. "What if she wants to marry someone else?"

Jerry paled. "That's why I can't give her a *get*, in case she ever wants to come back to me."

"But then you could just..." Sandy stopped as the realization hit her. "You're a *kohen*," she said.

"Yes," he said simply.

"But you should still give her a *get*," Sandy said. "She's not religious and she might just get married to someone else in court if it can't be done in *shul*. She won't realize the seriousness of what she's doing, and then she might have more children and then..."

Jerry buried his face in his hands. "Please don't say it," he pleaded. "I know there would be a problem with the children, because without a *get* a second marriage would be adultery. But I can't bear the thought that she could marry anyone else. She is my wife. I love her. I would do anything for her.

"I know that the way I treated her is unforgivable. I didn't realize how heavily the drink had gotten hold of me or how much of a monster I had become. I've only understood since going to AA. I've met people who have changed their lives completely and have stayed that way for years. Early on their wives or husbands left them, and they lost everything. But some of them have gotten back together.

"She put up with so much abuse that I don't blame her. But if we divorce, I will lose her forever. And I want her back so very, very much."

"You know, Jerry," Sandy said at last, "Elise couldn't possibly know how much you've changed. You have to meet her somewhere, somehow, as if by chance. I believe that if she saw you, she might well change her mind."

"But how? She won't see me, she refuses."

"I suggest we get Tanya and Richard to work on this. Elise goes out shopping. You could meet her anywhere. Tanya knows her schedule."

Jerry suddenly felt better. Perhaps something could be done.

He went to the door of Grandpa's room and knocked, saying he was ready to play Trivial Pursuit. Grandpa came out, rubbing his eyes. He had been away for most of the day, possibly on some kind of business errand. Sandy had long given up asking him. The two men were soon engrossed in their game, obviously enjoying themselves thoroughly.

Michael came in and transferred from the wheelchair to his favorite chair. His thoughts turned immediately to Stephen.

Stephen had been going to the Rabbi regularly, although the Rabbi tried everything to dissuade him. He had been to the *Beis Din* where he went through a rigorous questioning and had been told to "continue learning — it could take years." However, both the Rabbi and the *Beis Din* had urged Stephen to take a trip to see his mother and find out for certain what kind of Jewish ancestory he had. Perhaps there would be something in that. But it wasn't even certain that he had any Jewish ancestors at all.

Michael had a feeling that Stephen and Eva had already stopped seeing each other. They were both extremely idealistic.

Stephen had gone that day to visit his mother. Michael wondered what he would find out.

CHAPTER 24

I'm sorry, Mrs. Cohen, but we don't really have any jobs available that would suit you. You haven't worked for many years. Do you know anything about computers?"

"No," said Elise. "But I do know typing and shorthand, though it is somewhat rusty."

"Perhaps you should do a computer course before you look for a job. In this day and age one has to be computer literate. Not that I can guarantee you anything at all once you have equipped yourself. The job market is very difficult at the moment. Many experienced, efficient people are not able to find work."

Elise sighed. Several employment agencies had told her the same thing.

"You will need to know Word Perfect and of course Microsoft Word for Windows, and how to do a spreadsheet, and of course you have to have a fairly good working knowledge of Windows 95."

Elise nodded, not daring to admit that she had no idea what he was talking about. "If you do find someone who would employ me now..."

"I'm sorry, Mrs. Cohen, I don't think there is any chance of that. You could perhaps go to the stores and see about being a cashier, though the registers are somewhat complicated."

Elise passed a shop with mirrored windows and peered at herself, hoping no one was watching from the other side. Yes, she had an attractive face, even though her dark eyes had even darker lines under them, and her mouth had lost its "smiley" look which had so distinguished her as a teenager.

She made her way along the crowded street. Everyone seemed to be going to work. Why couldn't she? Did all these people know about Windows and Word Perfect and...what was that other Word-something he was talking about? Had the commercial world changed so much? Commercial world! They had pointed out to her very clearly that the commercial world was now the corporate environment. Would she ever learn?

"Oh hello, Elise! How good to see you! How are Jerry and the children?" Elise turned to face Linda, an old friend from school.

"I'm fine, thank you," she said a little automatically.

"And how are Jerry and the children?" the woman repeated.

"Oh I...I..." stammered Elise realizing that she was blushing. "I...I...." In spite of herself her eyes filled with tears.

Her friend looked at her with concern.

"Is there something wrong?" she asked. "Can I help you?"

"No," Elise said, trying to sound normal. "Yes, yes there

is." She took a deep breath. "Jerry and I are getting divorced."

"I'm sorry," Linda said, "I'm so sorry. Can we talk about it? Are you busy now? Can we go for some coffee?"

Elise was about to refuse and then thought better of it. She wasn't busy. She wished so much that she had something to be busy with.

Without even waiting for an answer, Linda was steering her towards a coffee shop. It was almost empty and very shortly they were both drinking steaming hot cups.

"It isn't that I don't love Jerry," Elise began. "I will always love him in a way. It is just...it is just that he was drinking so much. Maybe it is because I love him that I had to leave. I couldn't bear to see the ruin he was bringing on himself."

Linda nodded. "I can imagine," she said.

Elise continued, grateful for a chance to talk. She couldn't talk to her mother or to any of her family. They would just pour criticism and anger on Jerry for his behavior. They naturally took Elise's side, and Jerry was, in their eyes, a drunken monster who could do no good.

"I never realized that alcohol was a problem until it was really bad. He used to drink a lot but hold it very well. We had a bar at home which was always well stocked, and he would often take two or three, or maybe four, five, or six glasses, in the evening.

"The first time I became worried was when I found bottles hidden around the house. It was totally unnecessary because we had the bar, and it was always full. But I began to find bottles in the cupboard, both empty and full ones. I found bottles in the bottom drawer of his desk and in the garage and in the trunk of the car and...all over. I didn't think even then that things were really serious...and he was drinking so much that he would often pass out. If we went to parties, I would have to drive home. I was getting worried, though. I mentioned to him about the bottles, and then they would turn up in even more ingenious places: at the bottom of the laundry basket or far, far down in the bottom of the cupboard. It took years until it became such an obvious problem. I just hadn't realized it would get to that."

"Did you talk to him about it?" asked Linda.

"Yes, yes," said Elise, not being able to hold back the tears and hastily putting on her sunglasses so that no one in the shop would notice. "Oh yes. I begged, I pleaded, I nagged, I shouted, I cried, I did everything."

"Did it help?"

"Not at all, or perhaps once or twice for a day or so. But he would drink even more to escape, he said, from my constant nagging. What could I have done? I was becoming an awful person. It does that to you. What else, in the end, could I have done? I had to do something."

She was silent, sunken in her own misery.

Linda changed the subject. "Are you working?" she asked.

Elise became even more miserable. "I've looked for jobs and answered ads in the press, and I went to some agencies. I'm simply out of date," she said bitterly. "Windows and Word are just names to me, names I can't even remember. Today we are in a world of computers. I don't even know how to switch one on."

"That's something I could help you with," Linda said eagerly. "We have a computer at home. I could teach you all kinds of things. It wouldn't take you long. You know how to type already, don't you?"

"Not computer typing," Elise said, unable to emerge from her misery. "It's totally different."

"No it isn't," insisted Linda. "I've been working most of my life, except when the children were small. I switched over to computers and advanced with them."

Suddenly Elise realized she had focused only on herself. "Tell me how you've been," she said.

"There's nothing much to tell," Linda said. "You probably heard about Keith."

Elise stiffened. "No, I haven't," she said. "I haven't seen you since we left school."

"Well, Keith died," she said. "Three years ago he was killed in a car accident."

"I'm so sorry," Elise said, suddenly feeling guilty about her own pain.

"We were happy together, really happy, and it was all so sudden, so devastating. He didn't die right away. For weeks he hovered between life and death. But then he picked up an infection, and very shortly he was just...gone....

"I think that's why hearing about divorce hurts so much," she continued. "I can't explain it."

"But I have to divorce him," Elise said. "He is drinking so much. I can't take it any more."

"Do you miss him?"

"No...yes, of course I do."

"Perhaps he will stop drinking."

"Then I suppose I could just marry him again."

"People have done that," Linda nodded. "People have stopped drinking. They really have. I've seen some alcoholics make a real turnabout. There's a man at work. He was a very good worker but a very bad drinker, until just over three years ago. Then he got in contact with AA and has been a changed person ever since. Maybe he can help Jerry."

But Elise wasn't listening. Instead she had turned ghastly white.

"What's the matter?" asked Linda. "Are you all right?"

"I never thought of it before," Elise said. "Jerry is a *kohen*, he wouldn't be able to marry me again."

"Why not? " Linda asked, somewhat confused.

"Well, you see, he is a *kohen*. He can't marry a divorcee, and I would be a divorcee."

"But it's not the same. You were his wife."

"It makes no difference," Elise said, her voice raised in agitation. "If I divorced him I would lose him forever. And what would happen if he stopped drinking like this man you were talking about? It would be too late."

"So you could marry him again," persisted Linda, now totally confused.

"Linda, you aren't Jewish. You don't understand. Jerry is a *kohen*, a priest."

"Your husband is a reverend, a Rabbi?"

"No, no," she answered quickly. "No, he isn't at all. He isn't even religious."

"But how can you be a priest if you aren't religious?"

"Linda, you don't understand. You don't have to be religious to be a priest. You are born that way, just like you are born a Jew."

"But a person can become Jewish, can't they? I once knew someone who did that, so obviously you can study and become a priest."

"No, you can't. It's a family thing. You can't become a priest."

"Then if I became Jewish, could I marry a priest?"

"No," said Elise, still devastated by her realization that divorce would cut her off from Jerry forever. "A *kohen* can't marry a convert."

"But I heard that a convert becomes a full Jew."

"Yes, that's true, but she can't marry a *kohen*. He can't marry a divorcee or a convert, and I would be a divorcee."

"That's difficult for the convert isn't it?" Linda asked, a little offended.

"Linda, it is far more difficult for the *kohen*. He has all kinds of extra things he has to keep."

"Does Jerry keep them all?" Linda asked. "Didn't you say he wasn't religious?"

"He's not. But he still can't marry a divorcee."

"You really have a complicated religion," Linda said. "I would never be able to understand it."

"Well," said Elise, "you've helped me understand something very important. Now, would you really be able to help me with the computer?"

"I would love to," Linda said good-naturedly. "If you came over this evening we could start right away."

"Mom, don't you miss Dad?"

Elise was startled by her daughter's question. Why did she have to ask it so bluntly? Of course she missed Jerry, but there was nothing she could do about it, nothing at all.

"When are we going back home?" was her next question.

"Never!" Elise said emphatically. But as the words came out of her mouth she was struck by the fact that she didn't mean them, that somehow she was still hoping for a miracle.

"Mom, don't you like Dad anymore?" she asked.

Her tone was more insistent. Why was her daughter asking her such personal questions? On the other hand, Jerry was her father, and despite his drinking she loved him. "I don't like your father's drinking," she replied.

"But Mom, it was only the alcohol. It wasn't him. Was he drinking when you married him?"

"No, he wasn't, actually," she said. "It wasn't a problem then."

"Can't we give him just one more chance?"

Elise was silent for several minutes. "I'm sorry," she said at last. "I'm really, really sorry. But I can't do that. We have to start new lives."

"And live with Grandma forever?" her daughter asked.

"Of course not. We'll get a small apartment somewhere, an apartment of our own. It will be difficult, but we'll have to start all over again."

She turned away quickly before her daughter could spot the tears which had suddenly welled up in her eyes.

Elise Cohen pushed her shopping cart around the supermarket. She had to be careful how much she spent. Very careful.

She looked at the price on a can and put it back. They would eat something else; there was no money for luxuries.

She sighed as she made her way through the crowded store. Why had life been so cruel to her?

She remembered the early years of her marriage. Jerry had been her hero, and she had adored him. They had done everything together, traveled, played squash, run every morning at six, yachted, laughed, and cried together. Jerry had been her life.

Richard and Tanya had come, and Jerry was a loving father.

And then he had begun to drink — and a deep, dark shadow had been thrown across their home, never to leave.

She remembered with bitterness the long nights of waiting for him to come home, the fights, the words they both had said which had cut them to ribbons. She had tried hard to make the marriage work, for the sake of the children, but she could see the effect it was having on them.

She remembered the night she left. She hadn't been able to take it any longer. She felt that if she didn't leave and take Tanya with her, she would either go mad or burst into a thousand pieces.

Staying with her mother in her tiny apartment had been a relief at first, but then it had become difficult. But she couldn't afford anything else. She had been to the divorce lawyer, and the papers would be served within the next few days. And she knew, now, that as soon as the *get* came through, the divorce would be forever.

She wondered how Jerry would react.

The picture was somehow too painful to hold onto, and she was once again with the younger Jerry. If only that Jerry could be found again!

At that moment a tall man stepped in front of her shopping cart, blocking her way. A tall man with clear blue eyes which looked straight into hers, a person who looked extremely familiar, but very, very different.

CHAPTER 25

I t was good to see the sea again, to drive along the coastal road with the wind whistling through the car. Stephen drove straight through the night, stopping only for gasoline and Coca Cola.

He wondered if his mother would be surprised to see him. He probably should have phoned, but ever since his university days he had loved to surprise her, to see the expression of delight on her face as she opened the door to find him standing there.

But this time he was apprehensive. How could he tell his mother he was going to become Jewish? She had always claimed that although Jews were good people, they should be avoided as friends because they were "different." Different? The woman he loved and his best friend were both Jewish. They didn't seem different at all. But maybe, in some way, he himself was different. And, once, his mother had let slip that they had a Jewish relative. When questioned further she had brushed away the subject, saying that the person could hardly be called a relative. Still, he knew it was something to pursue.

He had had several chats with Rabbi Sandler and had quickly come to realize the authenticity and the depth of Judaism. He had developed an overwhelming drive to join the Jewish people. He dearly wanted to marry Eva, but he knew that conversion took months, if not years, and he could not expect her to wait for him.

He sent her a note saying he was converting but had received only a short message thanking him for letting her know. There were no promises that she would meet him again. But he could hope. He could surely hope.

When he first approached the Rabbi, he wanted to convert to make things right for Eva, and the Rabbi had told him certain things about *Yiddishkeit* and then gently pushed him away. It did not take long before he began visiting the Rabbi regularly, and both of them realized that the idea of converting had begun to stir his soul.

He wondered how he could put this across to his mother. She wasn't attached to her religion at all. But for her son to be a Jew? That was different. What was her attitude to Jews? It was not contempt. In fact, she had never actually said anything derogatory — nor anything positive. Her true feelings were a mystery, until a sudden realization overtook him. She seemed to be afraid of Jews! Why, he had no idea.

He was approaching Port Shepstone. Again he began to feel anxious. Perhaps he should have told his mother he was coming. Perhaps he should have discussed it on the phone with her. But he knew this was something too sensitive and too serious.

He drove through the shopping district and turned left,

driving up a steep hill. He remembered how as a youngster he had wished the hill was less steep. After his illness, his mother had even considered moving to make things easier for him. But he remembered begging her to stay. He wouldn't have traded their view of the sea for anything.

At that time he had felt it would be impossible to live away from the coast, and yet he had studied at the University of Natal and then moved on for his MBA to the University of the Witwatersrand Business School in Johannesburg. And then, except for his trips home, he had never left Johannesburg. He had found the apartment he was still living in and had accustomed himself to a scenery of buildings and mine dumps. At times he would pretend that his window faced the sea, that he would just have to pull the curtains to see the ocean: an inky green, with flashes of light reflecting the moon and stars and maybe the lights of a ship far out. Now he could see it all once again.

He drove up the hill almost to the top and parked outside the quaint, tile-roofed house which had been newly painted on the outside.

Opening the gate, he walked down the long garden path. His mother had always loved gardening. Rows of pansies greeted him along the path, backed by zinnias and irises, and bushes and bushes of roses, all sizes and colors and scents. It was good to be home.

He rang the doorbell, expecting his mother's usual cheery "hello." There was no response. But the windows were open and she would definitely be there, unless she had slipped out for a few minutes to shop.

He rang again, and then again. Eventually he heard his

mother's voice from inside saying that she would open right away.

She gave a scream of delight when she opened the door.

"Mum, why are you using a stick? Are you hurt?"

"It's just my ankle, Stephen. I sprained it. But it will be better in a few days. I was standing on a chair to change a lightbulb and somehow I must have slipped. The doctor came and had a look at it. He isn't really worried but says it will be painful for a few days."

"Where else did you hurt yourself, Mum?"

"Only on my arm — my shoulder, actually. It's much better already. It was only the day before yesterday that I fell."

"You should have waited till I came and fixed it for you."

She smiled. "Stephen, how on earth am I supposed to know when you are going to visit? You never tell me. I just hear this knock at the door and there you are. But it is always a wonderful surprise."

She started to hobble in, and he held onto her arm, leading her to the couch. "Sit there, Mum, I will make you some coffee."

"I'll do it son...but...I don't have any fresh milk. I was due to go for some but I couldn't actually get out."

He was already seated but he sprang up. "Give me your shopping list. I will go right now."

"No, please sit down. You can make me some lemon tea. Later you can get me some chickens. I know how you love chicken a-la-king."

"Actually, smelling the fresh sea air again, I have been craving fresh fish. And I will cook it myself. I have to have a special pan and I will buy that, too. I'll get you chickens to put in the freezer, but while I'm here I'll stick to fresh fish. Let's have some tea and we can talk." He busied himself in the kitchen, realizing that his mother lacked many more basic necessities. Thank goodness he had come when he did. She might never have managed.

She took the tea from him, watching him with loving eyes. Even though they lived several hundred miles apart, he was the pivot of her life.

"Why didn't you phone and tell me?" he asked with concern.

"I didn't want to worry you. I can manage like this for a few days. And, anyway, you came," she whispered. "I didn't even need to phone you."

He looked at her. She seemed to have aged over the past few months. He tried to work it out. He knew he had been born when both of his parents were getting on in years, when they had despaired of ever having a child. Yes, his mother wasn't young. It was just that she had always looked after herself, warding off an elderly look, which seemed to have descended upon her with the accident.

She asked the question which she had asked so regularly over the years.

"And so, Stephen, have you met anyone? You can't be a bachelor forever, you know."

"I did meet someone," he said quietly. "But I think it's finished."

"Finished?" she asked, a little shocked. "She liked you, didn't she?"

"Yes, she did, I'm sure she did. I think she liked me a lot. But it couldn't work, at least not now. You see, Eva is Jewish."

His mother blushed crimson and her hand began to shake as she put down her teacup on the table in front of her. Again that look, a look of...what was it? He was right, surely he was right. It could only be described as fear. "You didn't want to marry a Jewish girl?" his mother asked. "I think I can understand that." Her face was scarlet.

"No, no, I wanted to marry her. I desperately wanted to marry her."

"Stephen, this is the first time I have ever heard you talk that way. What is this girl like?" she asked.

"Mum, she is wonderful, beautiful, intelligent, caring...everything a man could wish for. But she is Jewish, and I am not."

The look of fear turned to one of terror. She could not speak, and she leaned forward to take a sip of her tea.

"Are you going to marry her?"

"I can't, Mum, she won't marry a gentile. She won't even go out with me anymore."

"Then why did she go out with you in the first place?"

"I don't think she expected it to get so serious. We were just friends, and then it became something more, and she just broke everything off, saying she could only marry a Jew. At first I didn't know what was making her so distant, but a friend, a Jewish friend, explained it to me."

"She hurt you!" said his mother, tears coming into her eyes.

"She hurt me and she hurt herself. But I just had to respect it. Now I have begun to understand why she could not marry me, why she could not give up any aspect of *Yiddishkeit* to marry a gentile."

"*Yiddishkeit!*" exclaimed his mother, again starting to tremble. "Where did you get such a word from?"

He stared hard at her. "Do you know what it means?" he asked.

"No," she said flatly.

He was silent.

"Though Yiddish is a Jewish language, isn't it?" she said. "It is best to leave all that alone. It would be better for you to find a nice gentile girl."

"Mum, you know that I have never felt anything for anyone else."

"There was Barbara," his mother almost snapped. She had always wanted him to marry Barbara, a fellow student from Natal University. In fact she, and Barbara herself, had set their hearts on it. But it hadn't worked with Barbara. There was no reason on earth for him to want to spend the rest of his life with her.

"I didn't want to marry her," he said. "Even if it isn't Eva, I will, myself, only marry a Jewish woman."

Forgetting her pain, she rose to her feet, winced, and sat down again. "You can't marry a Jewish woman," she said. "You are a gentile, a Christian. I sent you to Sunday School for years. You are a gentile."

"I'm converting, Mum. I'm going to become Jewish. It is not because of Eva, and I don't expect her to wait for me. It could take at least two years. But I'm convinced that this is the right thing to do, the only thing to do. I've been learning with a Rabbi, and it is like a great and beautiful world has just opened up for me."

"You are going to leave your religion for a woman?"

"Mum, I really don't think I've ever believed much of it. I wouldn't have gone to Sunday School unless you made me go.

"And I'm not converting for Eva. *Yiddishkeit* is much greater than that. I want to be a Jew because I love Judaism and I want to serve Hashem completely."

"What nonsense are you talking?" she said. "Such strange words!"

"Apart from you, Mum, the people who've meant the most to me have been Jewish: Raymond, who was so good to me in school after I was ill, Eva, and my best friend Michael. He is Jewish, in fact, he's even *frum*. And now I've met Rabbi Sandler and his family, a family where Hashem is a very real part of the household. Even the smallest child speaks about Hashem in a natural way."

"It is time for my soap opera," said his mother. "Please switch on the TV."

Stephen soon got bored with the romantic entanglements — bored, and perhaps a little hurt. Was there any possibility that Eva would wait for him? Perhaps if she saw how serious he was about conversion they might be able to meet again.

He went to his room. He was tired and lay down on top of the blankets, and drowsiness overcame him.

He slept for almost six hours, waking to find himself covered with a mohair blanket. It must have been very painful for his mother to reach the top of the cupboard to get it down for him.

Getting up, he could smell cooking coming from the direction of the kitchen. How was he going to tell her he was gradually beginning to keep kosher?

And why had his mother shopped for him with that painful ankle, when he had wanted to shop for her? He looked at his watch and gasped. Had he really slept that many hours?

Running into the kitchen, he found his mother sitting in front of the stove. Groceries were piled on the counter.

"Did you go out to the shops, Mum?" he asked in concern.

"No, no, I couldn't do that," she said. "I phoned up the corner store and explained what had happened, and that you were here, and I asked him if he had any fresh fish. He had some yellowtail that had just been caught, a fairly large one. He sent it over to me with some vegetables and other things I needed. You see, it was all delivered to my door, to my kitchen, in fact. He had chopped the yellowtail into several pieces; very convenient, it was. And now I will be able to feed my son as I have always done."

Neither made mention of Eva or the conversion. It was as if there was a mutual agreement not to discuss the subject. But he saw a strain in his mother's eyes which hadn't been there before, and she looked as though she had been crying. Perhaps she was in more pain than he had realized. But it was more than that, he was sure. And there again was the fear in her eyes. What was she so afraid of?

For the three days he spent there, not a further word on the subject was passed between them. But she was becoming calmer, and seemed possessed with a strange kind of determination that he could not understand.

It was the day before he was due to leave that she herself broached the subject, at the same time making it clear that she did not want to be asked any questions.

"I have something for you," she began, "something you can take to your Rabbis. It has nothing to do with me, only with you. For me it is all too late."

Only limping slightly, she went into her room and brought back a sealed envelope.

"Don't open it," she said. "I beg you not to open it. Just deliver it to the people in charge of your conversion."

He was amazed when he saw what was written on the envelope.

TO: The Rabbis, Johannesburg Beis Din.

How did his mother know anything about a *Beis Din*?

CHAPTER 26

I t has been really good to be with you all," said Grandpa. "But of course I can't stay here forever. I have to be getting home."

There was a unified cry of protest from everyone, even little Chanie. How could Grandpa leave?

"Well," he said, a little flattered by everyone's distress, "I do have a home to go to in the States. I do have things waiting for me."

"But," Sandy said, close to tears, "you don't have family there."

"I have a half-cousin in Boston," Grandpa said.

"When did you last see him, Grandpa?"

Grandpa looked a little sheepish. "Not for many years."

"Grandpa, what have you really got there?" she asked.

"Nothing, really," he admitted. "I have a few friends. I've retired, so I don't do anything special. It's just that I am used to it. I have my computer there, which I do a lot of work on."

"Grandpa, you have your computer here."

"Oh, yes? Where is it? My laptop has been missing since

I got home. I can't find it anywhere, and there was a terribly important e-mail message for me."

Sandy frowned. She remembered him asking about that, but she hadn't been able to do anything about it. Or had she done something? She couldn't really remember. "Please stay with us, Grandpa," she said again.

"It has been wonderful staying with you, poppet," he said. "But you have your family. I can't stay with you forever, and, also I...I need my independence and...."

"We can build you a cottage in the garden, and even attach it to the house if you want," said Michael.

"A Grandpa apartment," Grandpa said, wrinkling up his nose. "One day when I am old, perhaps...but not now. I would have no real freedom. I can't even stay out late without you sending...well, without you sending a helicopter after me."

Sandy looked to see if he was joking and was amazed to find that he wasn't. Thank goodness they had sent a helicopter after him.

Daniel was looking thoughtful. "Grandpa," he said. "You don't have to stay with us. You have enough money. You could just buy an apartment or even a house. Just find something in Johannesburg, really close to us."

Grandpa looked surprised. The possibility hadn't occurred to him.

"Daniel, that is something I will most definitely think about. In fact, the more I think about it, the more I like the idea. I could have my own lounge, computer room, library, just as I do at home."

"That would be wonderful," Sandy said. "I think that is the best idea."

"At least I will have a computer," he said.

"Grandpa," Sandy said. "Where could your laptop be? You didn't take it with you that night that you were taken to that house, did you?"

"Definitely not," said Grandpa. "I never took it with me to the bar."

"But it is missing," she said, "and it has been ever since that night."

"You couldn't find it when I phoned?" he asked.

Sandy thought for a moment, a look of horror on her face. Yes, he had asked her to do something, she remembered now. She had found it and she hadn't been able to.... No, no, wait, she *had* found it, yes. He had wanted her to go into his e-mail and save it to disk. She hadn't known how to do that, but she had printed it out for him, and...

Excusing herself, she ran out of the room, returning a few minutes later with several pages of printout. As Grandpa looked at it, a broad smile appeared across his face.

"William," he murmured as he read on, "we've got you. Now we can go to the police."

"Grandpa, I thought William was helping you." Everyone was confused.

"I suspected William from the very beginning," said Grandpa. "He obviously wasn't used to money, and he was very free with it. But at the same time, William didn't seem to really have it in him to be a true criminal."

"He was working with someone else?" asked Michael.

"Oh, I'm sure he was with this Martin. I am quite sure of that. Anyway, once William is arrested he will tell all about his partners. A pity, really. I was beginning to like him. He just got sucked in by his financial difficulties, and now he will go to jail."

"You feel sorry for him, Grandpa?" Sandy asked incredulously.

"Not really, poppet, I don't really. He is a criminal now, and he hurt my family. He hurt my grandson-in-law badly."

Michael was staring into space. "You mean..." he said, "you mean, my name might be cleared?"

"It looks like it," Grandpa said. "I will be in touch with the police now. But," he muttered to himself, "I can't get away from the feeling that this is much bigger than just William. I hope I am wrong."

The phone rang incessantly.

Michael was surprised to hear Stephen at the other end on a long-distance call.

"Could you please come with me to the *Beis Din* tomorrow morning at ten o'clock? I have made an appointment with them, and Rabbi Sandler has agreed to come also. I'll be back in the city just before ten and will pick you up from work.

"I explained to my mother about Eva, about the *Beis Din*, and about Rabbi Sandler. She cried a great deal but she wouldn't say why. She just gave me a whole lot of papers in a sealed envelope and asked me to give them to the *Beis Din*.

"I'm still not sure what it's about, but I'm beginning to have an idea."

Michael was excited, but he would have to wait for ten o'clock the next morning.

If he hadn't been so preoccupied, he might have noticed that Grandpa, too, was extremely excited now that he realized his e-mail, via Hong Kong, had been answered. He had taken the letter straight to the police.

Since Jerry had not come over to play Trivial Pursuit, Grandpa was playing Solitaire. Anyone looking at him would have noticed a slow smile cross his face ever so often.

But no one was looking.

It was 10:15 A.M.

Three Rabbis from the *Beis Din* were busy reading the documents which had been in the envelope Stephen's mother had given him.

They were mostly in Hebrew. Some seemed to be in Russian.

Occasionally they would hand Rabbi Sandler a document to look at.

As he read, his eyes glistened with tears.

Michael and Stephen sat quietly, watching the rabbis.

After what seemed an eternity, the *Av Beis Din* turned to Stephen.

"Stephen," he said. "Or rather, Shlomo, as these documents name you, there is no doubt that you are Jewish, completely Jewish. You have always been Jewish. Your mother is Jewish, your grandparents were Jewish, and your great-grandparents were Jewish, rabbis in fact," he added.

"The war broke out when your mother was eleven years old. She was the only survivor of her family. Like so many others, her life was in danger and she was 'adopted' by a Christian family. She learned their ways and eventually followed their customs, feeling everything was lost.

"She met your father and married him and brought you up as a gentile. But she could not resist, without her husband's knowledge, to do a *bris* for you, and name you Shlomo.

"She writes here that she was going to tell you about this one day, but she could never bring herself to do so, until you told her about Eva and that you were about to convert to Judaism."

Stephen felt he was dreaming. His mother was Jewish! His eyes shone as he realized the full implications of what the rabbi was saying.

Later, as they reached the foyer of the *Beis Din*, Rabbi Sandler turned to Stephen. "I will take Michael back to the office for you," he said. "The wheelchair will fit in the back of my car. I know that you have rather urgent business to attend to."

Michael frowned. What was he referring to?

But Stephen had disappeared.

CHAPTER 27

Well," Grandpa said, "this definitely deserves a celebration. Who will come with me?"

He looked a little crestfallen when he saw that everyone was busy with their pre-Pesach vacation activities. Sam and Dina were engrossed in a game that they were playing. Daniel was working with Zevi Sandler on a school project, something that had to be handed in right after Pesach.

"Where did you want to go, Grandpa?" Daniel asked tentatively.

"Oh, maybe Johannesburg Zoo, or Emmarentia Dam, or Gold Reef City or...or just anywhere."

"We'd *love* to go, Grandpa," said Daniel, Zevi echoing with a nod. "Maybe we can take our project with us and do some of it wherever we go. Maybe we can even go to more than one place — the zoo, and then the dam. But how are we getting there, Grandpa?"

"There are such things as taxis," Grandpa said. "You just aren't used to them. I suggest you check all this out with your mothers, and if they agree we can leave in about forty minutes."

★ ★ ★

"I'm sorry, but the mine is closed to visitors today. We only operate on the weekend and public holidays, or when we have a lot of visitors. We can't open everything up for just a few people."

Disappointed, Grandpa turned away with the two boys. They would go to the amusement park. There would definitely be *some* of the rides operating if not the major ones.

Zevi and Daniel tried to hide their disappointment and act cheerful. The trip down the mine was one of the main reasons they had voted to go to Gold Reef City. They would just have to wait till Sunday and join in with the regular crowds.

They went into the large exhibition hall.

"Look, here is a mine shaft reconstructed," said Zevi. "What a pity we couldn't have gone down the mine."

They walked through one of the houses that was furnished as in days gone by. Even the kitchen had appliances which were at least fifty years old.

Grandpa picked up a hand mixer. "These things worked so well. You had a chance to see cream beaten and changing into butter before your very eyes. It was harder work, of course, and took a very long time, but it was worth it.

"I remember how we used to get milk straight from the cow because we had to make sure it was not mixed with any milk from a non-kosher animal. Then we would skim off the cream and make butter out of it."

Daniel stopped short. "But Grandpa, you don't keep kosher at home now. Did you then?"

"Of course I did," Grandpa said.

"So, why did you stop?"

Grandpa turned to face the wide, inquiring eyes of both Zevi and Daniel.

"Well," he said, "well...it just sort of happened slowly, life in general and all that, you know." He looked a little uncomfortably at the two boys, who obviously *didn't* know.

"Excuse me, maybe I could be of help to you."

Grandpa turned around to see a tall, dark gentleman who was dressed in the uniform of Gold Reef City. He turned his full attention on the man who had rescued him from an awkward situation with the boys. There seemed to be something familiar about his voice, but he couldn't place it. Perhaps he had heard him speak the last time they were there.

"Excuse me, sir," the official said again. "Can I be of help? I was told you wanted to go down the mine. For a fee I can take you down there myself. I often do it privately." He chuckled a little to himself.

Grandpa was about to refuse when the boys started to jump up and down with delight.

"That would be *fantastic*, Grandpa, really fantastic," Daniel said. "It would be so exciting to go down alone."

Grandpa could find no reason to refuse. It was just a strange feeling he had. Where had he met the man before? It was almost as if he had met him somewhere in some kind of dream. But of course, that was quite absurd.

"Come, Grandpa," said Daniel, noting his hesitation.

"Are we going way down the shaft?" Grandpa asked.

"Only part of the way in," declared the man. "We will go down fast because there are only four of us."

In the large room used for changing into mine gear, the

man selected four mining hats, four coats, and four pairs of boots.

"Aren't we keeping you away from your other work?" Grandpa asked, still somewhat hesitant.

"No one will miss me for half an hour or so," he said. "I have often done this before." He set the lift in motion and they entered the rickety cage, Grandpa realizing again that his phobia of lift shafts had not left him. Perhaps that was the source of his nervousness. He closed his eyes for a few seconds, seeing in front of him the mass of tangled metal and people. Would that vision of horror remain with him forever?

"I think this will fit you," said the man, handing Grandpa a heavy waterproof coat. The man's hands seemed to tremble. Did he really know how to operate the machinery?

The shaft looked dark, and the man went over to the side of the room and switched on the lights. Grandpa tried to enjoy and forget about his fears.

"Can you imagine? Here we are, all alone. We will have the whole mine to ourselves!" Zevi sounded really excited. They kept switching the headlamps in their helmets off and on until Grandpa made them stop, saying they would waste the batteries.

They were soon speeding down the shaft, and Grandpa gave a sigh of relief when they landed.

It was strange being in the mine alone, without the voices of all the other visitors. They watched how the lights from their hats made eerie shapes all over the wall.

"It actually *is* a bit scary," Daniel said. "I mean, so many tunnels, and us here all by ourselves."

"Don't worry," said the official. "The way it is all mapped out you can't really get lost."

"But I've seen all sorts of tunnels with the old workings leading off from here, that the tourists didn't go along," Zevi said. "My father always makes sure we stay together."

The man took them along the regular tourist route and once again they saw the seams of gold and gold ore.

"Is this real gold?" Zevi asked, running his hand along a seam.

"Yes it is," replied the man.

"Can I chip out a bit to take home?" asked the boy.

"Better not," said the man. "You don't want to cause a rock fall or anything like that. This is one of the spurs, the offshoot tunnels. It isn't wooded up like the ones back there."

"But it looks like it would be so easy," said Zevi.

"I'll tell you what," said the man, with an attempt at a fatherly smile. "I'll let you follow a gold seam for a while and you will see how large it can get. It's a little out of the way of the normal route, but not very far."

With a key he opened a gate leading to a side tunnel. They followed him along the path, and he pointed to the craggy wall. "See over here?" he said. "We can all follow this. I will tell you when the seams begin to broaden out."

"It must be very valuable," said Daniel.

"Not really," the man said. "It isn't worth mining in here anymore. The labor is more than the price of the gold. We have found richer seams in other mines, so we have left this one."

They walked on and on, far from the usual tour route. Many tunnels had been dug out when Crown Mines were in their prime.

"I wish I could have just one piece," Daniel said, "just a small piece. If no one is mining, would it matter?"

To his excitement, the man replied, "I'll see if I can get a tiny chisel for you to use, but you may only chip off a thin sliver," and with that his footsteps echoed further and further away, until there was silence.

"I wonder what it would be like to work down here," Zevi said. "Imagine chiseling away at this rock all day, for years and years and years, and hardly ever seeing daylight."

"Well, I'm sure they had some kind of break," Grandpa said. "Maybe a day off a week. But you are right. They had to spend most of their waking hours right down here."

CHAPTER 28

As they emerged into the midday sunlight, Michael and Rabbi Sandler saw that the afternoon papers were already on the street. They stopped short as they saw the headlines:

"Two Men Arrested on Massive Fraud Charges"

It was the front-page article. Several companies — and Selby had been named — had been swindled out of millions over a period of nearly a year. The police asserted that with the help of one or two responsible citizens, they had traced everything to two men, Martin Greenfield and William Dougall. A clever trap had been set. The evidence had been overwhelming and irrefutable, sent from William's e-mail address.

His name was cleared!

"*Baruch Hashem*!" said Rabbi Sandler. "I knew this had to happen some day!"

Michael brought the paper to the office, placed it casually on the receptionist's desk, and walked into his office.

It was not long before almost the entire office staff had

crowded around to congratulate him.

Shortly afterwards, Michael received several phone calls from the executive directors saying they appreciated that he had not left the firm, even though suspicion had been focused on him. They also hinted at a raise in the very near future.

It was only later that Michael discovered that one of the "responsible citizens" who assisted the police in finding the real criminals was Grandpa himself. Grandpa had picked up a hint from Jerry's ramblings about the bar and had begun going regularly to the bar himself, where he had gained some leads and followed them up. At one time, Michael found out, Grandpa had even been working closely with one of the criminals and had caught him in a trap he had set up.

His name was cleared, and it felt good!

Michael's mood sobered somewhat when the police captain entered his office. He was alone, and he had lost the aggressiveness of his previous interrogations. He sat Michael down and looked at him seriously.

"First of all, I have to congratulate you," he said. "I know we gave you a rough time, but we were simply doing our duty. I'm happy you were not involved."

Michael thanked him. Was that why the policeman had come, to tell him this? By the man's attitude, he didn't think so.

"We thought we had this case wrapped up," said the captain.

"You mean, it wasn't those men?"

"It was them. Beyond a shadow of a doubt. We have interrogated them and they confessed fully."

"Then what else is going on?" Michael asked.

The policeman shook his head in dismay. "They were not working alone. At first William thought they were, but the whole thing is part of a very large syndicate of the most dangerous criminals."

"Isn't it good that you found this out?" Michael asked. "Isn't that good?"

"It's not so easy," the captain said. "We don't have many leads on them. Even William and Martin covered their tracks well. The only one who knows something about them is your wife's grandfather, and they have him apparently at the top of their 'hit list.' They want to silence him because he knows too much."

"He didn't tell us about all this," Michael said.

"And I'll tell you why," answered the policeman. "It seems he knows, but he doesn't know he knows."

"Have you asked him?"

"I can't get hold of him," the captain said. "He went out this morning with Zevi Sandler and your Daniel. No one knows where they went, and no one has seen them since."

"But Zevi's parents must know where he went. They are very strict about that."

"Zevi asked to go with your grandfather, but they were not sure where they would be going. It was to be either the Johannesburg Zoo, Emmarentia Dam, or Gold Reef City."

"How did they go?" Michael asked.

"By taxi to Gold Reef City, but they obviously didn't stay there long because hardly anything was open. My men looked there, and there was no sign of them. They must have gone somewhere else, but we have conducted intensive searches in all the other places. We are unable to locate them."

"I'll phone Grandpa. He has his cellular phone with him."

"We've tried that several times. All we get is the message: 'The number you have dialed is unavailable. Please call again later.' "

Michael's foot suddenly began to throb.

CHAPTER 29

You know, that guy has been gone a long time. Do you think he went all the way to the top?" Zevi looked puzzled.

"Yes he did, I am sure," Daniel said. "I heard the cage from somewhere in the distance."

"That means he really will be a long time. I didn't mean to make him go all that way for it."

Grandpa had become very quiet, very quiet indeed. A steely fear was beginning to lodge itself inside his stomach. There was something wrong, something desperately wrong. He tapped his inside pocket, pleased that he had brought his phone with him. Not wanting to use up the battery, he had kept the phone in "off" position. Now he pulled it out and switched it on.

"Grandpa, are you going to phone him?" Daniel asked.

"I will try to," Grandpa said, feeling a certain satisfaction as the green light of the cellphone went on. He waited for the signal that the phone was usable in the area. No signal appeared. "It's not going to work," he said. "We are out of range."

"But that can't be," Daniel said. "Last time we were in Gold Reef City it worked perfectly. You got a strong signal then."

"I know," Grandpa said, feeling his mouth go dry. "But we are pretty far underground, and that puts us out of range."

"We'll just have to wait until the man comes back," Zevi said.

They waited...and waited.

"We shouldn't waste our lights," said Grandpa. "Perhaps only one of us should keep his on at a time."

Zevi looked at him sharply. "You mean, you don't think the man is coming back?"

"I don't know," said Grandpa. "I just don't know."

"He must be," Daniel said. "He said he would be. He's probably looking for that chisel. He wouldn't desert us." Nevertheless both boys extinguished their headlamps and replaced their hats.

"Perhaps we should make our way back to the shaft," Grandpa said. "Maybe the phone will work from there."

They stood up and started to retrace their steps, silent in their anxiety. Had the man deliberately left them down there, and if so, why?

With only one light, the shadows were even more eerie. They plodded on and on.

Grandpa stopped. "We have a choice of two tunnels here," he said. "Which one do we go along?"

"Aren't we following the seam on this side?" asked Zevi. "I mean, I remember looking at it all the way along the wall before."

"That's right," Grandpa said. "Brilliant!"

They walked on and on, making sure to always stay with the seam.

"It seems much longer this way," Daniel said. "Are you sure..." He broke off as Grandpa stopped again. They could see why by the light of his headlamp. There was a metal gate blocking their way. They were in one of the tunnels blocked off from the tourists' part of the mine, and they were on the wrong side of the gate. Someone had fastened it securely.

They were prisoners.

"Maybe the phone will work here. We must be quite close to the shaft." Once again Grandpa pulled the phone out of his pocket and switched it on. The green light appeared, but again there was no signal. He turned it off, disappointed, but not really surprised.

"Actually, we must be very far from the tourist area," said Daniel. "That place has lots of lighting. Without Grandpa's headlamp we would be in pitch darkness."

Grandpa extinguished the light for a few seconds. Perhaps there was light further on. But no, all was black.

"Maybe you boys should shout and see if anyone can hear. Maybe this guy is still around somewhere."

They screamed and shouted till they were both hoarse, but there was no response.

"What do we do now?" asked Zevi. "Do we go back to where we were before?"

"Here we have some chance of being rescued by the next tourist party," Grandpa decided.

"The next tourist party?" cried Zevi. "Today's only Tuesday."

"And by Shabbos, when the first tourists arrive, we won't even be able to shout. We have no food and water, nowhere to sleep...nothing!" Daniel was becoming hysterical. "What do we do?"

"We say *tehillim*," Zevi said quietly.

"Okay," said Daniel. "Do you know any by heart?"

"Yes, I do," Zevi said, "and so do you."

"I do, too," Grandpa said quietly. "I think if you learn something like that very early you just don't forget."

It was a strange atmosphere, there in the depths of the earth, in total darkness (they had turned off the torch to save the battery). They were all fearful and anxious, but as they said *tehillim* they felt themselves surrounded and infused with a sense of peace. Grandpa brushed the tears away from his eyes, glad that no one could see him in the darkness.

"What do we do now, Grandpa?" asked Daniel when they finished.

"I'm sorry," Grandpa said. "I should have realized they don't organize individual tours down a mine. This is all part of what's been going on."

"But Grandpa, Mr. Dougall was caught. He confessed. It's all over."

"I don't think so," Grandpa said. "I think William and even Martin were only small cogs in a very big and ugly machine. I could never prove it or explain it, but I've had this feeling for a long time, ever since..."

"Ever since the night you were kidnapped, Grandpa?"

"Yes, I know I didn't get drunk that night. Something else happened, and it wasn't Martin and William who did it. There were other people involved. If only I could remember."

They fell silent. What else was there to say.

"Won't our parents try to find us?" Daniel asked.

"How would they know where we are?" Zevi said. "We told them the Johannesburg Zoo or Emmarentia Dam. They might even look for us here, but they certainly wouldn't look down the mine, especially when told that no one was allowed down today."

"That's true," said Grandpa. They had still not turned on the light and the darkness was almost tangible. "By the way, did anyone ever figure out what happened to my laptop?"

"I haven't seen it since you went away that night," said Daniel. "Mom said she put it on the dining room table but it wasn't there when I went to look for it. It just vanished."

"Was there anyone in the house at all that morning? Any stranger, that is," Grandpa asked.

"No," Daniel said, "definitely not. No one came by...except...but then I didn't answer the door to him, Sam did."

"Except who?"

"Oh some painter. He was already looking at our walls before Mom said that he was in the wrong house. She looked and he had some address down the road."

"So some painter has my laptop. Well, it is to be expected, I suppose. Anyway, what do we do now?"

"Maybe there is another way out," Zevi said. "I mean, do mines have only one entrance?"

"I don't think so," Grandpa said. "There could be other shafts, but in a disused mine, the cages wouldn't be working."

"But maybe the cellphone would connect there," Daniel said.

"We have to be careful. The underground is honeycombed with tunnels. We must not get lost."

"Maybe if we turn to our left all the time then we can come back by only turning to the right."

"It might not work," Grandpa said, "but I suppose we don't have much choice. We might get a phone signal somewhere else, especially next to a shaft."

"There were many passages leading off the tourist section," Zevi said. "Can't we get onto one of them?"

"We'll just come up against another gate and another and another. The gates are there to keep people from going down the passages. That man got a key and opened it for us, and then he locked it again. We won't get through."

Grandpa felt desperate. If they wanted to kill him down here, why did they have to trap the boys with him, boys who had their whole lives ahead of them?

"Let's go," said Grandpa. "Who will lead this time?"

"I will," Zevi said. "We'll go back to where we were before and continue from there."

"I'm going to do one thing," Grandpa said. "I'm going to tie my handkerchief onto this gate so that we can recognize it if we come back."

"What about the other passage?" Daniel asked.

"We'll try that next time," Zevi said. "Let's go this way first."

Almost automatically they followed the gold seam that grew wider and wider. Zevi suddenly stopped, giving a deep sigh. "It was my love of gold that brought this on us," he said. "I wanted a sliver of gold, and look where it brought us."

Despite himself, Grandpa laughed.

"Zevi," he said. "None of your family has a love of gold. Yours is the most caring family I've ever met. I have watched the way you all give and give and give of yourselves, of your time, and of your money. You don't have anything like gold fever...." He stopped short. "That's who he was! That's where I saw him, in the room where they poured the gold. That man had gold fever, an intense and destructive love of gold."

"What is gold fever, Grandpa, and who had it?" asked Daniel.

"I saw it in his eyes when the gold was being poured," continued Grandpa. "A man becomes a slave to his love of gold, to his need to obtain it at all costs. That's what Zevi and his family *don't* have," he finished.

"But who has it?"

"Our guide. The man who just left us. He was the man I saw. I thought I recognized him. He has gold fever."

Zevi was running his hand along the gold seam. "Such a precious metal so far below the ground. Hashem makes the most incredible things."

"And Hashem knows where we are," Daniel said. "And He can get us out of here."

"Absolutely!" exclaimed Zevi.

"Right," said Grandpa.

They reached the place where they had been before and sat down to rest, illogically comforted by a familiar landmark.

Some twenty minutes later they got up and walked on, following the same seam and picking up another one as that one ran into the ground. It was hot, and the perspiration was pouring off them. They walked for almost two hours, each time taking the left hand turn, every now and then stopping to rest and encourage each other. Zevi's torch was getting dimmer and they decided to use Daniel's.

"Thank goodness we only used one torch at a time," Daniel said.

"That means, though, that we only have a few hours of light left," Grandpa said. "I suggest we try to move along in the dark and only use the torches when we have to."

"I'm thirsty," Daniel said. "Isn't there any water any-where?"

"I don't know," Grandpa said. "I don't know. Sometimes you can find water but I don't know how good it would be."

"No one knows where we are," Daniel said soberly.

"Hashem does," said Zevi quietly.

The hours dragged by and they were becoming ex-hausted. These tunnels seemed to go on forever. Grandpa was up ahead now, leading the way through the darkness. They had decided the light was too precious to use when not absolutely necessary.

They were negotiating a particularly rocky path when they heard a bump and a low moan, and Grandpa sunk to the floor. Daniel immediately switched on the torch. Grandpa had hit his head on a protruding rock and seemed to have lost consciousness.

But no, he was talking, though his words were confused and garbled. "You have no right to take me like this," he was saying. "You have drugged me, I know you have. But I will not speak to you. You won't get any information from me. You tried to hijack me, to kidnap me. What do you want to know from me?" His next sentences were unintelligible, but he was obviously very angry about something.

The boys froze in fear. Had Grandpa gone crazy? What was he talking about?

"Are you all right, Grandpa?" Daniel asked.

"No, no, I am not all right," said Grandpa. "These people have drugged me to make sure I don't remember anything about this. They want to question me."

"What do the people look like, Grandpa?" Zevi asked.

"You can see them as well as I can," Grandpa said irritably. "Here is Michael's managing director, Mr. Caldwin, and here is the man with one eye smaller than the other. Did he have an operation on it? It almost looks a different color than the other one. As for this woman who gave me a lift...she is dark...her hair is tied back with a...with a... with...a...green... green...greeeee...."

At this point Grandpa seemed to fall asleep. Both Zevi and Daniel said a few *tehillim* and then shook him awake. "Grandpa, Grandpa. Are you all right?"

"Yes, of course, I'm fine. "

"Grandpa, can you still see those people?"

"What people?" said Grandpa, looking around. "Where are people?"

"Who is my father's managing director?" Daniel asked.

"Oh, he is someone I've known for many years. Mr. Caldwin. He is not just the managing director of the bank. He is a multimillionaire in his own right. He actually owns several firms. What makes you talk about him now?"

Realizing they were only going to confuse him, they dropped the subject.

"Are you all right, Grandpa? How is your head feeling?"

"Well...it is a little sore...it...Wow! I really have a good bump, don't I? I must have hit my head on something."

"Do you want to stay here, or should we move on?" Daniel asked.

"I suggest we move on," Grandpa said, standing up gingerly. "No, I do feel peculiar. Maybe we should rest here for a while." They had put on the torch and its light cast gloomy shadows around them. They could not even see a gold seam. They switched off the torch. It was warm and dry, and slowly, out of sheer exhaustion, they fell asleep.

Zevi was the first to wake up. He switched on the tiny light in his watch and looked. It was already 6 P.M. He should daven *minchah*. He woke up Daniel.

"Isn't it too late for *minchah*?" Daniel asked.

"I don't know, " said Zevi. "But it will really make us feel better."

Grandpa was stirring, and he sat up, obviously feeling better, too. "We must move on," he said briskly. "We must go as soon as you finish davening. I really wish, sometimes, that I had the kind of faith you boys have."

"Grandpa, you just have to start doing things that connect you to Hashem. That's what my teacher says."

"And I must stop doing things that push me away, such as eating *treif* and breaking Shabbos."

The boys were silent. Grandpa already knew all the answers. What could they say?

They continued along the passage, every so often lighting the torch to see that there were no obstacles or protruding rocks.

"Hey, Grandpa, where are we? We are coming out into a big room." Daniel grew excited.

"This is another station or gathering place or whatever they call it," Grandpa said. "It probably hasn't been used for years. There must be another disused shaft here somewhere."

It was not difficult to find. They flashed the torch up, and up. The shaft seemed to go on forever.

"Can I climb up there?" Zevi asked.

"Definitely not," Grandpa said. "That is totally impossible!" He shuddered.

"Let's try the phone, Grandpa. Maybe it will work here."

Again Grandpa switched on the phone. The green light appeared and then a faint outline of a signal, which quickly gave way to the "no signal" sign.

"We almost got a signal there," Grandpa said. "If only we were a little higher. I think we are far too deep here. But there was something."

"I'm climbing up," Zevi said. "And I'm taking the phone with me. We can put in the number for your home so that I just have to press the green button and get right through. I'll come straight down, I promise. It looks safe enough if I don't go too far. There are things in the wall that I can hang on to and where I can put my feet."

Grandpa shook his head and then made a gesture of resignation. Did they have a better choice? He entered his home number, then Zevi took the phone from his hand and within seconds was climbing up the shaft. Grandpa felt dizzy watching him.

Zevi climbed and climbed, afraid to look down. He carried the telephone securely in his inner pocket. But he was hardly prepared for what happened next and nearly lost his grip.

The phone rang!

Pressing the green button, he answered it.

"Who is that, who is that?" came Sandy's voice. "Where are you?"

"It's Zevi," he said, realizing from the interference on the line that the connection was very bad. He spoke quickly:

"We are trapped down the mine at Gold Reef City. We are close to another lift shaft. You need to go down the mine and through the tunnel which is blocked and has Grandpa's handkerchief tied to the gate. Follow the tunnel, keeping left all the way. Bring the police and...

Zevi heard a noise above him and, to his horror, he saw the cage come hurtling towards him through the shaft. He climbed hastily downwards, knowing there was no way he could get out of the way in time.

CHAPTER 30

I got them," Sandy said, quickly writing down all the instructions. "They are trapped down the mine at Gold Reef City. Hurry up. Please hurry up. Just before we were cut off I heard Zevi scream!"

"I will send my men immediately."

"I am going, too," said Michael.

"What?" cried Sandy. "You can hardly walk. Please, Michael. Stay home with the children. Say *tehillim* with them, Michael. I'll go."

"I'm sorry, ma'am," said the policeman. "There might be violence. I don't want a lady around if there is shooting."

"I want to go with you," Sandy said. "I want to see that they are safe. And Rabbi Sandler will want to come, too. He'll be here any minute to pick up his daughter, Chaya. She can stay with the other children until he comes back."

"Okay, the Rabbi can come, and you can also come along as long as you keep a safe distance," the policeman acquiesced. "And Mr. Berman, if anyone asks, don't say anything about the phone call or where we have gone. There might be other people out there wanting to know."

★ ★ ★

"The cage, the lift, it's coming down!" Daniel screamed. "What will happen to Zevi?"

Grandpa had turned a ghastly white and was trembling from head to foot. "I don't know," he said. "Perhaps there is a space somewhere in the wall, an alcove where he can hide."

They could hear the cage making its relentless course towards them until, suddenly and noisily, it came to a stop somewhere far above them. Great grandfather and grandson stood there frozen as a shaken Zevi emerged from the shaft.

He ran towards them. "The cage stopped on the level above us, *baruch Hashem*!"

"Let's get out of here," Grandpa gasped, "in case the cage comes all the way down. We can't take a chance. We don't know who these people are."

They found the entrance to their tunnel, but Grandpa stopped short. "Let's take another one," he said, "and not go too far along. They may search for us in this tunnel because that's where they left us. I have a feeling we must hide, and hide fast."

They found an entrance to another tunnel and moved into it.

"Did you hear the phone ring?" Zevi asked. "I was so surprised I nearly fell down the shaft."

"Did you manage to speak to anyone?" Grandpa asked anxiously.

"I spoke to Daniel's mother," Zevi reported, still somewhat out of breath. "Though I'm not sure if she heard anything. The connection was bad and her voice was really faint."

They were silent as they heard the cage stop on their level, and they moved further back as the place was flooded with light. Five men were moving towards the tunnel they had just left. One of them seemed to be their captor. They waited till they could hear nothing.

"Let's take the lift up to the surface," Daniel whispered. "No one seems to be in it."

"No!" Grandpa said. "No, we can't do that."

"Why not?" asked Daniel. "We can leave the men in the tunnels like they left us."

"I don't know," said Grandpa slowly, hoping he wasn't being influenced by his own fears. "None of us know how to operate the cage and it must be years old. It stopped on the next level up, so there must be men there that we'd have to pass and maybe more at the top. As long as Sandy heard Zevi say the mines at Gold Reef City, we are sure to be all right."

They walked on a fair distance into their tunnel and sat and waited. If Sandy had heard the whole of Zevi's message, these men would bump right into the police. They would just wait and see.

"I'll stay near the Art Shop close to the entrance," Sandy said. "There are plenty of people here. It is quite safe." Indeed, the festive atmosphere of a regular evening at Gold Reef City seemed miles away from the drama that was unfolding beneath them. People were oblivious to the policemen and Rabbi Sandler entering the cage with an official and hurtling down the shaft at high speed.

"They can't be down there," the official protested. "The mine is only open on weekends and public holidays."

The captain ignored his comment. They hit the tourist level with a bump and got out.

"We're looking for a tunnel," he said. "It has a handkerchief tied to the gate."

The men were silent. There were several tunnels running off from the central gathering place. Leaving a man to guard the cage, the police spread out to search the tunnels.

Soon a policeman signaled that he had found the handkerchief. The official opened the gate, and with powerful flashlights, the men began moving down the tunnels.

"I think we should go further in," Daniel said. "What if the men come to look for us when they see we aren't where they left us?"

"What if the police never find us," Zevi said.

"What if the police don't even come," Daniel said soberly.

They were getting stiff in one position, however, so they all voted on moving. They walked slowly, agreeing to keep to the right, this time following a really magnificent gold seam. Entranced by it, they quickened their pace. Maybe they were heading for the first station. Maybe the police would be there. Hope spurred them on.

After an hour they came to a place where the tunnel joined up with a larger one. And then they saw the lights. It was those men! If they looked down the tunnel, they would surely see them. It was impossible to hide. They switched off the headlamp and waited.

Zevi suddenly gave a cry: "Tatty!" he said. "Oh Tatty!" Father and son were in each other's arms immediately.

"Your mother is waiting up there," the policeman said to Daniel. "Your granddaughter," he said to Grandpa.

"Come into our passage and turn off the lights," Grandpa told the police. "There are some dangerous criminals in this tunnel."

They obeyed immediately.

Zevi piped up, "And maybe one of them is the managing director of Mr. Berman's bank, a Mr. Caldwin."

"No, no," said Grandpa. "I would recognize Mr. Caldwin anywhere. He definitely wasn't with them."

"But you said, Grandpa. You said he was one of the people who kidnapped you."

"I what?" exclaimed Grandpa.

"Thank you, young man," said the captain. "You'll explain later. I suggest you four just remain here until we fix up this gang. We'll meet them quietly and surprise them. Thank goodness we met you first, otherwise they would have seen our light and escaped. I want you four to go further back into the passage." He opened a bag and took out three cokes and some halvah. "Mrs. Berman sent these for you," he said.

"*Baruch Hashem*," said Daniel. "We sure are thirsty. It's been like a fast day." He suddenly remembered, "And we have a lot of work to do on our projects. They have to be ready right after Pesach."

"I can hear them," whispered the captain. "We'll take them by surprise."

The men's voices were clear, even though they were speaking quietly.

"Find all three and see that they're silenced forever. We

can't afford to let that old man remember what he saw that night. The drug he got might dull the memory, but you can't rely on it totally. And if he remembers, we're sunk. Kill the old man and the boys on sight. I don't know why you didn't do it before."

The captain sprang out in front of them and blinded them with a powerful flashlight. They were quickly arrested and led off through the tunnels.

Dina sensed that something was wrong. "Daddy, where is Mommy?"

Michael tried to reassure her. "She has gone to find Grandpa and Daniel and Zevi."

"But where did they go?" Dina asked.

"Oh they..." He stopped suddenly. Surely he could tell his daughter. Why did there have to be such secrecy?

"Oh, I know," said Dina, noting his hesitation. "I know exactly. They went to the mountain to find that snake that bit you."

Michael laughed. "Do you think they would be able to find the right one?"

"Are there more there?" asked Dina in horror. "There can't be."

"Dina," Michael said, "I think it's time for you and Chaya to go to bed. It's really getting late."

"But Daddy, we are all so busy."

"What are you all so busy with?"

"Oh, working," said Chaya matter-of-factly. "We're working very hard."

The expression on her face made him suspicious. "What

are you working on?"

"Sam is painting."

"That's nice," Michael said. "When he's finished his picture he can come and show it to me."

Dina blushed. "He couldn't really do that."

"Why not?"

"He can't bring it. It's too heavy."

Michael's suspicions were increasing. "What exactly is he painting?"

"The door," Dina said softly. "The door to our room. We needed it to be a different color."

"Where did you get the paint?" he asked as casually as he could.

"Oh, in the garage. It was your paint, the paint you used on my tricycle."

"That was bright red," said Michael, "and there wasn't enough to paint a door."

"But there was also some white and we mixed it together and..."

"Ask Sam to come here *at once!*" Normally he would have marched over himself, but there were two steps down to the bedrooms which were difficult for him.

The doorbell rang.

"Please answer that for me, Dina.... No, no, you better not," he said, looking at her hands more closely. "Your hands have paint on them. I can't have the front door messed up."

The doorbell rang again. Michael moved into his wheelchair and went to answer it. He was amazed and honored to see Mr. Caldwin, one of the managing directors of his division of the bank.

"Mr. Berman," said Mr. Caldwin, holding out his hand. "I had to come here personally to tell you how gratified I am that your name has been cleared and to congratulate you. I consider you a valuable and loyal member of our staff. I think we should have a drink together."

Michael obliged, wheeling himself over to the cabinet to fetch two glasses and managing to pour out two drinks.

"How is your leg?" Mr. Caldwin asked. "Are you able to walk on it?"

"Oh no," said Michael. "It's really painful. I've been going to work in a wheelchair."

"So I've heard," said the man. "That must make you feel trapped, no? I mean, if anything happened you couldn't really get away, could you?"

"No, I couldn't," agreed Michael, a little puzzled. "But why should I want to get away, and from what?"

"Just a thought," said Mr. Caldwin, smiling. "I mean, if someone wanted to take you as hostage or something."

Michael frowned and Mr. Caldwin laughed at his odd joke.

"Is your wife at home?" he asked casually.

"No, no she isn't. She went to..." He suddenly remembered...but surely he wasn't expected to keep the secret from someone as distinguished as Mr. Caldwin. "She went to..."

"She went to the mountain to get Grandpa and the boys," Dina said, coming into the room. This time it was obvious she had been painting with Chaya and Sam. Her hair was splattered with red and white paint, and her hands were red and white, shiny, and wet.

"Oh hello, young lady," said Mr. Caldwin. "Whom have I

the pleasure of meeting?"

"Dina Berman," said Dina. "We are busy painting the door."

"Maybe you had better run along and finish it," said the man, a little irritably.

She muttered something about a lot of paint being stuck on the edge of the door and ran out. Michael hated to think what the whole thing was going to look like. What on earth would Sandy say? But he couldn't do anything at this moment, while he was entertaining Mr. Caldwin. How considerate of him to have actually paid Michael a visit at home.

"How is the family?" asked Mr. Caldwin.

"Very well, thank you," Michael said.

Mr. Caldwin stared at him. "Your wife's grandfather," he said. "I heard he had an unfortunate experience on Saturday night."

"How kind of you to ask," Michael said, genuinely impressed. "Yes, he did have a rather traumatic experience. He seemed to have had one too many at the bar, and a stranger had to take him home."

"Goodness me!" exclaimed the man. "Did he phone you when he woke up in a strange house?"

"Yes, fortunately he had his cellular phone on him and he phoned us the next morning."

"How did he know where he was? I mean, if he had just woken up in a bed."

"Oh, I think Vodocom, the telephone network, found him."

"They couldn't trace the exact address, could they?" asked Mr. Caldwin.

"No, he was traced to Boxburg."

"Boxburg is a large area."

"Well, we got a helicopter, the Gold Reef City one, and he signaled to it and we picked him up."

"Very neat," said Mr. Caldwin, a little dryly. "Gold Reef City, an interesting place."

"As a matter of fact," said Michael, and then he stopped. But what could be wrong with telling Mr. Caldwin?

"Does your grandfather know where he was, and who picked him up?"

"As a matter of fact, he doesn't," Michael said. "He remembers being offered a lift, but he doesn't remember the people, and everything after that is a complete blank."

"Interesting," said the man. "Couldn't you trace the occupants of the house where he was found?"

"Apparently that's taking a long time," Michael said, "but the police are working on it."

"I am sure they are," the man said grimly.

"Can I get you another drink?" Michael asked.

"Yes, yes, if you could. Or, rather, I can get you one."

"Don't worry," Michael said, wondering how to explain that Mr. Caldwin could not touch the wine in the cabinet. "A little exercise is good for me," said Michael, once more wheeling himself to the cabinet. "What would you like this time?"

"Maybe you have something sweet, such as a liqueur."

As Michael turned to him he caught a look of such chilling hatred that he quickly looked away, his hand shaking as he brought back the bottle. Surely he had imagined it. After all, the man had come to visit him on a mission of goodness from the bank. But couldn't he just as well have visited him at his office? Why at home on a weekday night?

Feeling decidedly uneasy, he pushed his chair opposite Mr. Caldwin's. The man was looking very unpleasant. Michael wished he would leave. But then, there was no way he could get him to leave, and, as the man said, there was no way he could escape. These words seemed to be eating at him. He pulled himself together. Why was he feeling so paranoid?

He was startled by the children shouting for him. "Daddy, Daddy, come quickly! Sam is stuck on top of the door. He can't get down and Chaya is trying to help him and it is getting worse because...."

"I'll go," said Mr. Caldwin. "I can get there quicker."

Before Michael could object, he rushed into the passage where the bedrooms were. There was silence, then squealing from the children, then the door banging, then more silence, and then kicking, more children screaming, angry shouting from Mr. Caldwin, and then two shots and silence.

Michael was painfully making his way as quickly as possible towards the sounds. It was extremely difficult to maneuver the steps but he somehow did it. He was relieved to find all three children standing, trembling, beside the closed bedroom door. It looked more like a cake iced with mayonnaise and ketchup. Rivulets of paint were pouring down the sides. There was still banging and shouting from the other side of the door.

"I'm sorry, Daddy," Sam said.

"Come here right now. Tell me what happened."

He felt relieved when they ran over to him. They helped

him renegotiate the steps, and he led them back to the dining room.

"Tell me, who fired those shots?" Michael asked. "Was it a real gun?" He was still shaking from head to toe, as were the children.

"Well you see, Mr. Berman," said Chaya Sandler, "that man wanted us to go into the room with him, and Sam was trying to get down from the top of the door, and then the door slammed on its own."

"Where is Mr. Caldwin?" Michael asked.

"He is in the room," Dina said miserably.

Michael was still puzzled.

"And we can't open the door," said Sam.

"Why not?"

"Well you see...the paint...."

"But the gunshots," said Michael. "Who did he shoot at?"

"Well, there are two holes in the door. That's why we couldn't keep trying to get the door unstuck because we could have gotten shot."

"Heaven forbid," said Michael.

"He kicked the door and then shot," said Sam.

"And of course the windows are burglar barred so he can't get out there," Michael said, trying to swallow his anger when he realized the children could have been shot.

He wheeled himself over to the steps. He could hear the man hurling himself against the door.

"I am sorry, Mr. Caldwin," Michael called out. "I will get someone to open it for you, but I can't take the risk of anyone being shot, and I myself can't help you in my condition," he said. "I will make a phone call."

"I have already made one," said the trapped man. "People are coming now to let me out, and then we will see.... I see you have your windows barred like all good South Africans. Maybe we can file through those." He finished off with a few choice words.

All four sat in glum silence, punctuated by the banging on the door as Mr. Caldwin threw himself against it.

Suddenly all attention was riveted on the front door as the key turned in the lock.

Sandy, Grandpa, and the boys piled into the house. Before anyone had a chance to speak, the captain called to Michael from the driver's seat of the police van, saying that he had to pick up at least one more dangerous criminal who seemed to be the mastermind behind everything.

Sitting in his wheelchair in the doorway, Michael shouted back to him: "Oh, Captain, could you help us out, just for a few seconds. My managing director is stuck in the children's bedroom."

"I'll send someone soon," the captain said. "What I have to do now is extremely urgent. We are going to have a lot of trouble finding this man. He has probably already escaped in his private plane."

"Then I'll tell Mr. Caldwin help is coming soon," Michael said. "How long will they be?"

At the mention of the name, the captain was out of the van and in the house, together with several of his men.

"Mr. Caldwin is the very man I am looking for," said the captain.

"He has a gun," Michael said. "Be careful.... I can't believe it, I really can't believe it." Michael suddenly burst into peals of laughter.

Rabbi Sandler had followed Sandy and Grandpa into the house.

"Mr. Caldwin is here?" they all exclaimed.

"Locked in the kids' bedroom," Michael said through his laughter, which had now become a little hysterical.

"But who did that? How did you catch him? How did you know to catch him?"

"Chaya, Sam, and Dina caught him," Michael said. "But we really didn't know who we had caught. It was quite by accident."

They laughed as they realized that even the police were having a difficult time trying to unstick the door. They eventually got in, and after one or two more wild shots from the captive, they emerged with a somewhat disheveled Mr. Caldwin. His clothes were full of red and white paint and even his hair was stuck with a blob of red. It all would have made him look very comical had it not been for the expression of total hatred on his face.

It was late the following afternoon when the captain again came to visit. He had a satisfied look and had obviously "wrapped up" the case.

"I came to return this," he said, taking Grandpa's laptop out of his briefcase. "It seems to be untampered with, though they probably looked at all the information on it."

Grandpa, still extremely pale from the events of the previous day, cradled it in his arms like a baby. "I sure am pleased to see this again," he said. "But stay for coffee and tell us what happened."

"You have no idea how much I would love some," said the captain, sinking into a chair. "We have been up half the night on this, and we've made several arrests. This time we have the top men, the core of the organization. It is all much wider than Selby. It stretches into the worst kind of crimes."

"Please tell us what happened from the beginning," Sandy said. "There are so many blank spaces, so many mysteries."

The policeman relaxed further into his chair as he started to eat the large slice of chocolate cake placed in front of him.

"Start with William Dougall," said the captain. "He was an intelligent young man, working in the bank, operating on an extremely tight budget. He was always owing money and was constantly in overdraft. He met Martin, a teller, a puny member of the larger organization. Martin did much of the hands-on fieldwork. There were several 'Martins' operating for hefty payments at various branches of the bank. Their job was to find people to work with, at the same time keeping their work disconnected from the main stream of operations. But it all was part of one large diabolical organization, with Mr. Caldwin as the head.

"Being a managing director of the bank, he was involved in a lot of the actual bank work and could oversee the illegal transfer of millions of rands taken from unsuspecting clients. How many of us actually take the time to check our bank statements?

"Michael had typed in figures that obliterated the record of the money taken from the Selby account. William had not done his job as well as he should have, and the withdrawals were not well concealed. The organization tried to keep all their transactions as veiled as possible, but it was not done in this case, and, of course, Michael made an excellent scapegoat.

"William found an interesting and unique way to 'hack into' accounts. He had apparently asked for assistance, though not directly, through the newsgroups on the Internet. He was answered by a professional computer hacker called Jip, who posted straight to William's e-mail address and provided him with the software he needed. He then found out what William was doing by getting into the hard drive of his PC, and he started to blackmail him for the money he had gained on the deals.

"Grandpa somehow realized this was happening, sent off his own 'blackmail e-mails,' and was answered by William, who thought he was, as usual, e-mailing Jip."

"But who *is* Jip?" Grandpa asked.

"We don't know," said the captain. "We are not even looking for him. He could be any person — male, female, old, young — anywhere in any country in the world, living and operating out there in cyberspace. There are many Jips. They are ahead of us with all the tricks.

"William's e-mails incriminated him, and, of course, he gave us every bit of information he had as soon as he was arrested. When we arrested Martin, he, too, spoke to us, though it took time to get him to 'open up' completely. We knew, then, that there were others and that this thing was much bigger than we ever imagined, but we didn't know who the kingpin was. In fact, Martin didn't seem to know, and

William definitely didn't know."

"But why did they kidnap Grandpa?" Sandy asked.

"Grandpa was becoming dangerous. He was asking questions all over the place. They wanted to question him and see how much he actually knew. They used a drug, Dormicum, which makes a person talk but at the same time makes him forget everything he said. They took him to a 'safe house' in Boxburg, still registered in the name of a deceased estate so as to be almost impossible to trace. The plan was to leave Grandpa abandoned in the house."

"For how long?" asked Grandpa.

The captain didn't answer. "Or maybe even worse," he continued. "After he escaped, everyone was working at top pitch to eliminate him. They saw their chance when they observed him leaving the house with the two boys. They followed...and you know the rest.

"They knew of a disused shaft where they could go down and meet you in the tunnels. Fortunately for Zevi, they stopped off at the wrong level before they reached the one you were on. Little did they know what their mistake cost them."

"How did they find us?" Daniel asked. "Those tunnels went on for miles."

The captain gave a cough. "Well, you were actually going around in rather large circles," he said.

"Amazing," said Grandpa. "Truly amazing."

CHAPTER 31

It was the first night of Pesach.

Michael looked around at his Seder table, gaining *nachas* from each person present.

On his left were Jerry, Elise, Richard and Tanya, their eyes shining with their newfound family unity.

On his right was Stephen, or rather, Shlomo, his fiancee, Eva, and his mother, who was gazing at the candles, a faraway expression in her eyes. She had journeyed in for the Yom Tov to celebrate her first real Pesach since the war had started, so many decades ago.

Mr. and Mrs. Wolfson and their two sons were also there. Grandpa had found several errors in Mr. Wolfson's accounting system, and it was obvious that someone had been tampering in his business. Without connection to the Selby printout, investigation had pointed clearly to his previous accountant, who had "feathered" his personal accounts with Wolfson money. He had quickly been apprehended and the money returned. The business was no longer in crisis.

Sandy was sitting with Daniel, Sam, and Dina. Grandpa had baby Chanie on his lap, and she was desperately trying to take his glasses off his nose so that she could try them on. He had found a town house in a nearby complex and was finalizing the arrangements to buy it. He knew, now, that he would never be able to leave this family.

Michael himself felt a sense of peace. But it wasn't just that his name had been cleared, or that the office had presented him with a gold-plated engraved pen and pencil set. Or that he had walked several steps unaided and without too much pain.

It was something much deeper. It was something to do with his commitment to *Yiddishkeit*. Regular learning sessions had made a tremendous difference — he had begun to grow again. Sandy had also begun to learn regularly, and he saw the change in her. It was also the fact that they had really begun to spread their *Yiddishkeit.*

Something which he had thought was dying now felt alive and growing within him. The changes were inner ones and had come about quietly and slowly.

Sam stood up and, in his clear high voice, began to ask the Four Questions.